DOCTOR-PATIENT COM...
ACCORDING TO

When your doctor says	*it really means*
"You might feel a little pressure here."	The delivery truck in front of the hospital, all ten tons of it, is going to roll over you.
"This might sting a little."	Have you ever been bitten by a large animal with very sharp teeth?
"This might pull a little."	Prepare for your kidneys to be yanked up to your throat.

"His funniest book . . . it will strike a responsive chord in anyone who ever has come face to face with a gimlet-eyed surgeon who is about three payments behind on his Mercedes."
—Atlanta Journal and Constitution

"Lewis Grizzard should be awarded a Pulitzer . . . the best book of his career . . . . Lewis Grizzard is funny. But he also has the ability to start you laughing, and while you are in the middle of a good belly laugh, change directions on you. He can leave you open-mouthed and with a tear in your heart."
—Chattanooga Times

"Grizzard can make you laugh from the belly and a moment later you will suddenly get misty . . . one way or another, his writing will touch you."
—San Diego Union

"Un-put-downable . . . about one laugh per line."
—Alabama Magazine

Lewis Grizzard

They Tore Out My Heart and Stomped That Sucker Flat

WARNER BOOKS

A Warner Communications Company

TO:

Dr. Thorne S. Winter III, Dr. J. Willis Hurst,
Dr. Ellis L. Jones, Dr. Charles R. Hatcher, Jr.,
Dr. Stuart J. Toporoff, Dr. Dave Davis,
Dr. Chilton F. Thorington, Rev. Gilbert Steadham,
Nurse Mary German, and a cast of hundreds more
in the Cardio-Vascular section of
Emory University Hospital.

Warner Books Edition

This Warner Books edition is published by arrangement with
Peachtree Publishers Limited, 494 Armour Circle, N.E.,
Atlanta, Georgia 30324

Warner Books, Inc., 666 Fifth Avenue, New York, NY 10103
A Warner Communications Company

Printed in the United States of America

First Warner Books Printing: June 1986

10 9 8 7 6 5 4 3 2

Library of Congress Cataloging-in-Publication Data

Grizzard, Lewis, 1946–
    They tore out my heart and stomped that sucker flat.

    I. Title.
PN6162.G785 1986   818′.5403   86-5542
ISBN   0-446-37039-8 (U.S.A.) (pbk.)
        0-446-37040-1 (Canada) (pbk.)

Introduction

This is the tale of two hearts. . . .

I

Murmurings
and
Sad Love Songs

I'VE HAD TROUBLE with my heart for as long as I can remember. Somebody keeps breaking it. I saw one of those public service announcements on late-night television. It offered some sort of pamphlet to young women who needed to learn how to say "No."

Can you imagine that? Young women today have to write off to Washington for a pamphlet in order to learn how to say "No." I thought it was something they were born with, like their inability to parallel park.

Girls never needed to look in a book to learn how to turn me down. Take when I was in high school. Those were timid, simpler times. All I wanted was to get kissed, but girls with whom I went out had a never-ending supply of excuses not to kiss me.

"I have a cold," was one I heard over and over. For years, practically every girl I cornered in the back seat of a 1957 Chevrolet had a bad cold. I started carrying around my own aspirin and orange juice. It didn't help.

Another excuse was, "I don't want to smear my lipstick."

"Go ahead and smear it," I would say. "Helena Rubenstein is a personal friend of mine."

My all-time favorite excuse for not kissing me was, "I don't want to get into trouble."

Don't want to get into trouble? Was I asleep during biology class? You can "get into trouble" just by kissing?

The only way I ever got around all this was when I went to college and began to use a wily technique known as "practice kissing." Here is how that worked:

"Let's kiss," I would say to my victim, "but it will just be for practice."

"For practice?" she would ask.

"Sure," I would continue, "we'll kiss, but it won't count. We'll do it just to see what we need to work on in case we ever decide to kiss for real."

One particular evening it took a young Phi Mu and me nearly 450 practice kisses before we finally got it right.

It was a friend of mine, Ronnie Jenkins, who taught me my first real lesson about women, which was, you never can tell about women.

We were between our junior and senior years in high school and we thumbed to Myrtle Beach, South Carolina, because we heard there were, in fact, fine young women there and you could buy beer legally at eighteen, which meant if you were sixteen, like us, you could even order it in a loud voice.

The best accommodations we could afford upon our eventual arrival at Myrtle Beach was the utility room behind The Waves Motel. We paid a woman who had no teeth two dollars a night for the privilege of sleeping amongst the discarded lounge chairs and deflated beach balls. There was no air conditioning, of course, but one side of the room was chicken wire, which allowed a soft, ocean breeze to creep in, not to mention the gnats and mosquitoes.

Our first night there, we were into modest involvement with two young women when a strange thing happened. A man, obviously very drunk, came out of nowhere and began climbing on the chicken wire that was one side of the utility room.

"Eileen!" screamed the man. "Are you in there, Eileen?"

We asked the two girls and neither was named Eileen, which was some relief to both of us.

"I'm looking for Eileen," insisted the man, now fully suspended on the chicken wire.

"I'll lean over and you can kiss my . . . " Ronnie began before I stopped him.

"Careful. Maybe he's got a gun," I said.

"I don't care if he's got a bazooka," said Ronnie. "Look what I've got."

From somewhere in the rubble of the utility room and in the dark of the interrupted moment of passion, Ronnie had found a large oar. He drew back with the oar and hit the chicken wire with great force. The man flew off the chicken wire and into the yard where he began to roll.

"Wilmington," Ronnie said the next day. "Wilmington, North Carolina."

"What's Wilmington, North Carolina?" I asked.

"Where that sucker on that chicken wire stopped rolling after I hit him with the oar," Ronnie laughed.

The two girls. They are what this story was to be about in the first place. We'd met these two girls on the beach, and what can you tell about girls? They asked us how old we were and since we were sixteen, we said we were nineteen. I was a sophomore at the University of Georgia, Ronnie was home on leave from the Marine Corps.

They said they were fifteen.

When we left Myrtle Beach, they gave us their address and phone number and told us if we were ever in Star, South Carolina, be sure to look them up.

Soon, Ronnie got the itch for another trip.

"Let's go see those two girls we met at Myrtle Beach," he said.

We raised thirty–two dollars between us, which was enough for a pint of Stillbrooks bourbon at the local Moose Club, if you knew the bartender, two one-way tickets on the Southern's Piedmont from Atlanta to Greenville, thirty miles southeast of Star, and three dollars left.

We ran through the Stillbrooks and spent $2.75 on Coke to mix it with in the club car of the train. When we arrived in Greenville, all we had was a quarter.

We started walking.

"Our troubles are over," said Ronnie all of a sudden.

"Our parents are here to take us home?" I asked, wishing out loud.

"No, stupid," said Ronnie. "I see a pool hall. Watch me work."

He was good at pool, Ronnie. Moved quickly around a table with confidence and finesse. Shot with one eye closed and the other watering from the smoke from his cigarette.

He fished our last quarter from his pocket and got into a game in no time. Eight-ball. "Let the kid break," said Ronnie's opponent. I didn't like the man instantly. He had several tatoos on his arms and the toes were cut out of both his shoes and his fingers were yellow from the miles of Camel smoke that had oozed between them.

Quarter a game to start. Ronnie was on a roll. He was up a dollar. Then, two dollars. Then, three. I'd never been inside a pool hall before. When the regulars began to whisper and the man with the tatoos began to perspire and light one Camel off the other, I didn't know it was time to be concerned for our lives.

Ronnie understood the situation perfectly. After he'd sunk the eight-ball in the right corner on a beautiful two-bank, he pocketed the last of the five ones his stick had brought forth from the table. And, just before the victim of Ronnie's immense talent was about to bring forth some blood from Ronnie's head with his own stick, Ronnie calmly asked the man, "Sir, do you have a daughter?"

"I ain't got no daughter," said the man.

"Too bad," said Ronnie, still calm. "If you did and she had your looks, I hoped we could shoot one more

9

game to see who enters her in the hog show at the county fair next year."

The man was too full of rage to move for the split second it took Ronnie to grab me and have us six blocks away from the pool hall and gaining on downtown Greenville.

"Make a man mad enough," Ronnie said, "and it's as good as landing the first punch. He's too stunned to move."

Genius. Ronnie Jenkins was genius.

We ate a couple of cheeseburgers and bought a six-pack with the money Ronnie had won, and then we called the two girls in Star and they said their parents would be out of town until two o'clock in the morning and they couldn't wait to see us, and would we bring them each a Hershey bar? Ronnie's wanted nuts. Mine, plain.

We bought the Hershey bars with the last of the money and hitched a ride to Star, which was a small place. We eventually wound up on the girls' front porch about ten o'clock. Nothing was moving inside.

"Maybe this isn't the place," I said.

"It's the place," said Ronnie, "they're just bashful."

When banging on the door and shouting didn't work, Ronnie started singing some Beach Boys' songs we had all listened to earlier at Myrtle Beach. Lights flicked on around the neighborhood, and that's how he finally flushed out the girls.

"We didn't think y'all would really come," said Ronnie's girl from behind the screen door of the house.

"Even brought the Hershey bars," said Ronnie. "You nuts or plain?"

"Nuts," she said. "Nadine is plain."

Now, the girls are eating the candy bars behind the screen door and we're still on the porch.

"Can we come in now?" Ronnie asked.

"Y'all can't come in," said Ronnie's girl, the chocolate from her Hershey bar clinging to the side of her mouth. Neither one of them looked quite as pretty as they had at the beach, I was thinking to myself.

"Can't come in?" Ronnie burst out, unbelieving.

"We ain't old enough," said the girl.

"You're fifteen," said Ronnie.

"Naw, we ain't," the girl insisted. "I'm thirteen, but Nadine ain't but twelve. We lied to y'all at the beach. If daddy came home, he'd kill us and call the law on y'all."

Ronnie tried to get what was left of the Hershey bar back, but the girl had bolted the screen door and had already eaten all the nuts anyway. I looked in one more time to see if I could get a last glance at Nadine, but all I could see was her back. She was feeding something to a cat. Probably the rest of her Hershey bar.

We were down after that. No girls. No money. We caught a ride with a brakeman on the Southern, who was heading back to Greenville, and he let us off at an all-night service station where Ronnie managed to get his arm up a vending machine and pull down two packs of toasted malted crackers for us to eat.

We sat there all night, waiting for the dawn when

11

we'd hitch back home. Ronnie was quiet that night, deep in thought.

Just before daybreak, he turned to me and said, "I'll bet that won't be the last time either one of us gets made a fool of by a woman."

Genius. The man was a genius. And a prophet, as well. I'm thirty-five now, and I've been married three times, already, which is even more of a feat when you consider I didn't start until I was nineteen.

The first person I married was my childhood sweetheart. Lovely girl. Blonde. Sweet. I got fat eating her cooking. We lasted three years.

My first divorce, when I was twenty-two, was terrible. I was heartbroken over the entire matter, and for the first time in my life, I turned violent. Luckily, nobody was injured, however. My wife moved out and took an apartment. One night, I decided to go visit her and beg her to come home. Not only did I love her and miss her, but I didn't know what to do about my underwear, which is a problem that befalls a lot of men when they divorce for the first time.

When I was a child and wanted a clean pair of underwear, I would go and look in my drawer, and there would always be clean underwear. Same when I was married for the first time. When my wife left me, my underwear no longer marched from where I dropped it, washed itself in the washing machine, and then marched back, folded itself, and returned to my drawer.

Nobody answered when I knocked on the door to my wife's apartment. Suddenly, it occurred to me she was out with another man. I returned to my car in the parking lot and waited for them to come home. I would confront them both, I decided, and tell my wife of my love and she would come back to me and I would have clean underwear again.

I also decided she could be out with Dick the Bruiser, for all I knew, so I went to my trunk and got my tire tool. I waited for several hours. My wife and Dick the Bruiser never came home. I went to sleep with my tire tool in my lap. The next day, I found out my wife hadn't been out with Dick the Bruiser, or anybody else. She had been home visiting her mother.

I felt like an idiot, having spent the night with a tire tool. I went to the laundromat and washed my underwear.

Three years later, I married again. We were in a terrible hurry to get it done. I called another friend of mine, Ludlow Porch, and asked if he would find a preacher as quickly as possible.

"Consider it done," he said.

The preacher had a small, thin mustache and talked in a squeaky voice. He looked like a crooked Indian agent off "Tales of Wells Fargo." He began the service by opening the Bible and squeaking out, "It says here. . . ."

Three years later, when I divorced my second wife, Ludlow said, "I knew it probably wouldn't work out anyway."

"How did you know that?" I asked.

"Because I couldn't find a real preacher for your wedding on that short of notice. The man that married you changes flats at the Texaco station near my house."

I would have taken a tire tool to my friend Ludlow Porch, but he is built like Dick the Bruiser.

My second wife left me when we were living in Chicago. I had no alternative but to attempt to have dates with northern women. Since I am a native Georgian, I had never been out with northern women before. There are some distinct differences between northern women and southern women.

Southern women make better cooks than northern women. Northern women make good cooks only if you like to eat things that still have their eyes, cooked in a big pot with asparagus, which would have been better off left as a house plant.

Southern women aren't as mean as northern women, either. Both bear watching closely, but a southern woman will forgive you two or three times more than a northern woman before she will pull a knife on you. Most important, southern women know how to scrunch better. Scrunch is nothing dirty. It is where, on a cold night, you scrunch up together in order to get cozy and warm. And, southern women can flat scrunch.

With this attitude, it is easy to see why I was usually very lonely in Chicago. One night, I found a bar in Chicago with a country music juke box. I had a few beers and watched a guy walk over to the juke box with a handful of quarters.

My second wife had split and I was far from home, adrift on a lonely sea.

"Play a love song," I said to the guy at the juke box.

I needed it badly. One thing about country music. It has something to say.

The guy played a song entitled "She Tore Out My Heart and Stomped That Sucker Flat."

I left the bar and went home and washed my underwear.

* * * *

I was fifteen the first time I found out I had trouble with my heart that didn't relate to falling in or out of love. A country doctor listened to it beat and was not pleased with what he heard.

"Hmmmmm," said the doctor, moving his stethoscope to another position.

I didn't know it at the time, but a patient can learn a great deal about his condition simply by listening to the sounds the doctor makes while he conducts his examination.

"Hmmmmm" means there is something very interesting going on inside you. A policeman makes the same sound when he pulls you over and there is an empty bottle of Gallo Thunderbird wine on the seat next to you.

"Ahhhhhh" means he just remembered the last time he heard something like what is going on inside you. It was back in medical school the day he was assigned his first cadaver.

"Oooooh" means that, compared to you, the cadaver was in good health.

"What is the problem, doctor?" I asked.

"Heart murmur," he answered.

"What is that?" I asked.

"Nothing to worry about," he said. "You'll probably grow out of it."

I didn't worry about it. I went right along with the normal life of the next demented child. I played sports throughout high school. I went off to college and took up drinking beer and smoking cigarettes. I had other physicals.

"Hmmmm" is the sound doctors would always make when they listened to my heart.

The diagnosis was always "heart murmur. Nothing to worry about. You'll probably outgrow it."

I didn't outgrow it. Came time for me to leave college. It was 1968. Recall the unpleasantness in Vietnam that was raging at the time? The government was insistent I go and take a part. I had another physical.

"Ooooh," said the doctor.

I didn't have a heart murmur any more. The murmur, or strange sound emanating from my heart, turned out to be something else.

I was twenty-one. The diagnosis was aortic insufficiency. Doctors can spend hours explaining. I can do it much more quickly:

In the normal heart, the aortic valve—from which blood leaves the heart and goes out into the rest of the body—contains three leaflets, or cusps, which open when the blood is forced out and then close tightly together so that none of the blood can leak back inside the heart.

16

The doctor's diagnosis was that I had been born with only TWO leaflets in my aortic valve. I was born in 1946, right after the Big War. Perhaps there was a shortage of aortic leaflets.

Regardless, each time my heart pumped blood out, some of the blood would seep back into my heart, causing the "murmur" sound. On the next beat, my heart would have to pump that much harder.

"It's like taking three steps and then falling back two to make one," the doctor explained.

I was frightened, of course.

"You can forget the service," said the doctor. "They'll never let you in with an aortic insufficiency."

I wasn't frightened after he said that. Better an aortic insufficiency than a bullet from a Russian-made AK-47 right between my eyes, I figured.

The doctor made it quite clear to me. No big problem at the moment, he said. A young heart can withstand a great deal.

"But someday," said the doctor, "someday, you will have to have that valve replaced."

Someday. To a young man who has fallen in love in a motel utility room in Myrtle Beach, South Carolina, who has practiced-kissed Phi Mu's, and who has just been given a reprieve from the mud and blood of Vietnam, someday never comes.

II

"This Might Sting a Little"

I AVOIDED any big deal concerning the malfunction with my heart for the next fourteen years. The fact I had been diagnosed as having this "aortic insufficiency" caused a problem here and there with life insurance rates, but other than that, it was nothing more than a slight nuisance in the back of my head. Something to worry about only if I didn't have anything else better to worry about.

I took up tennis when I was twenty-three and quickly shed the fifty pounds I had gained eating my first wife's cooking. I could play three sets of hard singles in the hot sun, drink a half-case of beer, and still manage to dance an evening away, even if somebody else usually had to drive me home.

Symptoms of a problem with my heart? What symptoms? Someday, the doctor had said. . . .

* * * *

"Quit shaking the bed," my third wife said to me one night. It was late January 1982.

"I'm not shaking the bed," I answered.

"You're shaking it," she insisted.

"Go to sleep," I said.

"How can I sleep with the bed shaking like this?" my wife demanded.

The bed *was* shaking. I looked under the bed. There used to be things that slept under my bed when I was a kid. Godzilla. Zombies.

There was nothing under my bed but the banana sandwich I hadn't finished the night before. Godzilla wouldn't eat a day-old, half-eaten banana sandwich.

"I think it's your heartbeat," my wife said. "Your heart is beating so hard, it's shaking the bed."

That's nonsense. There I was, lying quietly in my bed. How could my heart be beating hard enough to shake the bed?

"You had better go to the doctor and get that checked," my wife said.

I had learned to all but avoid doctors since I was twenty-one. I had gone in for a few routine physicals, but there had been no new developments regarding the fact my aortic valve leaked.

Someday. . . .

"Do you really think it's my heart beat that is shaking the bed?" I asked my wife again.

"I don't remember installing a Magic Fingers system in the mattress," she said. "Go to the doctor."

I made an appointment at 3 P.M. with my doctor. I also made a date for a tennis match at 5 P.M.

I packed my tennis gear in the back of my car. Two

racquets. After you have played tennis for at least ten years, you can carry around two racquets. I drove away from my house, headed for my doctor's office. My greatest concern was whether I'd be able to get in and out of the doctor's office in time to make my five o'clock tennis match. Women. Sometimes, you have to humor them.

I knew something was wrong when my doctor's nurse complimented me on the shirt I was wearing soon after I had been given a chest X-ray.

"Hey," she said, "that's a sharp shirt you're wearing."

The shirt wasn't sharp at all. It was an ugly, green shirt I had won in a tennis tournament. Actually, I hadn't won the shirt at all. They gave everybody who played in the tournament a shirt and all the reds and blues were gone when I went to pick out my shirt.

"I really enjoyed your last book," the nurse continued.

How long did I have, I wondered? Six months tops? They're never this nice to you in a doctor's office unless they know something you don't.

My doctor is a quiet man. He's never ruffled.

"OH, MY GOD!" I heard him scream from the X-ray room.

I said a prayer. Lord, I said, don't make me suffer for long.

My doctor came back into the room where I was waiting in my ugly, green shirt.

"Hey," he said, "that's a sharp shirt you're wearing."

"Give it to me straight, doc," I demanded.

"Come with me," he said.

My heart was pounding hard enough to shake an entire Holiday Inn.

He put two X-rays up on the screen. One was the X-ray that had been taken of my heart two years previous. The other was an X-ray that had been taken of my heart in the previous twenty minutes.

"This is your heart two years ago," said my doctor, "and this is your heart now. Notice how much larger your heart is today than it was two years ago."

I can explain that, I said. I quit smoking and I've been getting plenty of exercise. That would certainly account for why I now have a big, healthy heart, rather than the undersized little fellow I had two years ago.

"I'm afraid you don't understand," said the doctor. "Your heart has enlarged. I would say about a sixth. This is quite dangerous."

He explained further.

The aortic valve leaks. Blood seeps back in. The heart is then filled above capacity. It must pump harder to rid itself of the blood. But it is fighting a losing battle. The leak is apparently bigger now than ever. The heart is pumping harder than ever. The heart is a muscle. The harder it works, the larger it becomes. The heart becomes too large, it can't function.

"And?" I asked.

"And you suffer heart failure and you die," said my doctor.

I asked for a couch and a six-pack. I settled for a hard chair and a glass of water.

24

My doctor explained some more:

The pounding heart beat that had shaken the bed was classic for my condition.

"Cross your legs," my doctor said.

I crossed my legs, right over left. My right leg bounced up and down with my pulse.

"Look at the pulse in your neck," he said.

Bam! Bam! Bam! The arteries pounded out of my skin. They call that "pistol pulse."

My blood pressure. The range was wide. Again, classic for my condition.

Still, I had suffered no shortages of breath. No chest pains. No dizziness when I was sober.

"That will come," the doctor said.

I didn't want to ask the question, but I asked it anyway.

"What can you do to repair this?"

"In a word?" the doctor asked back.

"Keep it as simple as you can," I said.

"Surgery," he answered.

There would have to be more tests, he said. He even suggested, if I so desired, that I get a second opinion. He also said the situation wasn't critical . . . yet.

"You might be able to avoid surgery for a time, with some help from drugs and a change in your lifestyle," he went on, "but there's no doubt you're gong to have to have a new valve eventually."

Change in lifestyle. No tennis?

"I wouldn't recommend you play tennis until we know more," he said.

25

I asked if I could use his phone. I called my opponent I had scheduled for five o'clock.

"I can't make tennis today," I said.

"How about tomorrow?"

"I can't make that, either."

"How about next week?"

"Nope."

I was fighting back the tears.

"So when can you play?"

"God knows."

"You okay?"

"Nope."

"What's the matter?"

"Someday."

"Huh?"

"Someday. It finally came."

* * * *

My doctor sent me to another doctor, and that doctor listened and felt and poked and prodded and ordered more tests. I took the standard EKG and then I took something called an Echocardiogram where they send sound waves into your heart, and when they had done all that, they still didn't know much more than they had known before, so they scheduled me for a cardiac catheterization.

I didn't know what cardiac catheterization was, so I had to be a smart aleck and ask.

26

"Before we perform the new heart surgery in this country," one of the doctors explained, "we first put the patient through cardiac catheterization. It is the best diagnostic tool we have available to us.

"We will insert catheters—little tubes—into an artery and a vein, and we will send them into your heart. We will inject dyes through the catheters so that we can take movies of the heart and of the arteries around your heart so that we can determine whether or not there is any blockage.

"This way, we can determine exactly what is your problem, we can see exactly how your heart is functioning, and we can tell if there are any hidden problems we didn't already know about."

That didn't sound so terrible, but doctors tend to leave out details when they are explaining things.

Friend of mine called me a few days before I was to have the catheterization.

"Had it myself a couple of years ago," he said.

"How bad is it?" I asked.

"Not too bad," he said. "First, they whack open your arm and start shoving all these tubes up in you. When they get the tubes in, they shoot in the dye.

"The doctor will say, 'This is going to burn a little.' What he doesn't say is where it burns."

I never learn my lesson. I had to ask where it burns.

"Your testicles," he said. "The dye goes from your heart to your bladder and burns your testicles. You'll think your testicles are going to burn right off. But try not to think about it before you go in there."

As my wife was driving me to the hospital to have my catheterization, she asked, "Something's been on your mind for days. What is it?"

I thought it best not to tell her.

Aside from the evening I was born, I had never been a hospital patient before. First, they make you put on one of those silly gowns with no back. Those gowns have no backs so it is easier for the nurses to slip up behind you and give you a shot in your hip.

"This is going to make your mouth very dry," said the nurse as she gave me a shot in my hip. A lot of things puzzle me about medicine. One is, if they want to make my mouth dry, then why do they give me a shot in my hip?

Next, you have to sign a release saying it is okay for your doctor to do this cardiac catheterization thing to you.

"Just sign it," said the nurse.

"But I think I should read the release first," I said.

"Just sign it," said the nurse.

Like I said, I never learn. I read the release, all the way down to the part where it said, in large letters, that cardiac catheterization includes "THE ULTIMATE RISK OF DEATH."

"Nobody said anything about dying from this," I said to the nurse.

"It's just a routine release," said the nurse. "I told you not to read it."

I asked for the number of the nearest cab service.

"You can't leave now," the nurse insisted. "I've

28

already given you a shot. What are you afraid of?"

"I'm afraid my testicles will get burned off and I will die," I said.

Before I could get out of my hospital gown and back into my clothes—you wouldn't have much luck hailing a cab with a bare bottom, I decided—they came to take me away for the catheterization.

They were bringing in another victim as I left the prep room. A nurse handed him his release.

"Just sign it," I said to him.

"But shouldn't I read it first?" he asked.

"Not unless you think you can catch a cab half-naked," I said, as they rolled me away.

* * * *

The first thing I asked the doctor, once I had been strapped down on the platform that poses for a bed in the catheterization room was, "How much is this going to hurt?"

"You are hardly going to feel a thing," he answered.

The next thing I asked the doctor was, "Have you ever undergone this procedure yourself?"

"No," he answered.

Just as I thought. He's going to cut open my arm on the other side of my elbow, stick tubes into my heart, inject dyes that will burn my testicles, and I am hardly going to feel a thing.

There is, in fact, this awesome communications gap

between the medical profession and its patients when it comes to pain.

I happen to be an expert on pain. I can get hurt pouring a glass of milk.

To me, pain is anything even slightly uncomfortable that is caused by somebody other than myself poking, picking, sticking, or jabbing me.

Pain to the medical profession probably would be something like cutting off your left foot without first giving you an aspirin.

The next time you're having something done to your body by a doctor, ask him, "Is this going to hurt?"

He will likely answer, "It might sting a little."

Sting is a word they use a lot in medicine. *Sting*, to me, means a slight pain, a level or two under a mosquito bite.

When a doctor says, "This might sting a little," he really means, "Have you ever been bitten by a large animal with very sharp teeth?"

Here are some other phrases to be careful of the next time you go to the doctor or spend any time in the hospital:

—"You might feel a little pressure here." This means the brakes on the delivery truck full of frozen pudding that is unloading in front of the hospital are about to give way and the truck, all ten tons of it, is going to roll over you. That's the "little pressure" you're going to feel.

—"This might pull a little." They used to say the very same thing to enemies of the state just before they put them on the rack. If a doctor says, "This might pull a

30

little," prepare for your kidneys to be yanked up to your throat. I'm no expert on the anatomy, but your kidneys have no business in your throat.

If you happen to be in the hospital or at your doctor's office and somebody mentions something about something "pulling a little," run as fast as you can for the nearest bus, even if you are half-naked.

—"I did this same thing to a seven-year-old boy this morning, and he didn't even whimper." Had the child been conscious, however. . . .

—"Now, that wasn't so bad, was it?" Not if you're used to finishing third in ax fights, no.

—"Very few of my other patients even complain about this procedure." That doesn't surprise me at all, Dr. Quincy.

—"This may tingle a bit when the needle goes through the nerve." Look around for a soft place to land.

—"I think the anesthetic has had plenty of time to take effect." Couldn't we wait just six more weeks to be sure?

—"If you will just relax, this will be over before you know it." Be especially careful of this one. The doctor is just trying to buy time before you start trying to hurt him back. What he really means is that the British fleet can turn around and sail all the way back home from the Falkland Islands and this tube will still be stuck straight up Argentina.

I am strapped onto the bed. The room is out of the Mad Scientist. I am wishing they had put me to sleep for this. They don't put you to sleep for catheterization

31

because there are times when they want you to cough and hold your breath. All they can do, I suppose, is make your mouth dry.

"One thing before we start," said a nurse. "If your nose itches, don't try to scratch it. We want you to lie still. If your nose itches, ask me and I will scratch it for you."

Why did she have to say that? My nose hadn't itched for years. As soon as she said not to scratch my nose, it started itching. It itched during the entire two hours of the procedure.

You can get somebody to scratch your back. You can get somebody to scratch your head. Your nose is something else. Only the person who owns the nose can adequately scratch it.

The catheterization. They deadened my right arm with shots of Novacain before making the incision. There are no nerves inside the heart, so there was no pain involved with the tubes. I felt the shots all the way down to my fingers.

The dye.

"This is going to burn a little," said the doctor.

"For God's sakes, go easy, man," I said.

I thought about cursing, but there were ladies present. I made a horrible face as the intensity of the heat from the dye reached its peak at the precise point my friend had indicated.

"Your nose itch?" asked the nurse.

"It's not my nose, and it doesn't itch," I answered.

All this time, they are taking pictures of my heart and my arteries.

"If you look on the screen," said the doctor, "you can see what's happening."

Doctors, of course, enjoy seeing a man's heart being tugged and pulled like it was a strip steak about to be flung upon the grill, but I close my eyes even when I get a haircut. I didn't choose to see what was happening.

I must admit there was very little actual pain involved with the catheterization, save the moment the doctor yanked the last tube down my arm and out through the incision. It felt like he was bringing my entire shoulder with it.

"Oops," said the doctor when I howled in anguish. "Oops" is not something you want to hear a doctor say.

They rolled me out of the catheterization room and into another room where the doctor took four stitches to close the incision in my arm. I had a tremendous desire to use the restroom at this point. The dye *had* gone to my bladder.

A nurse brought me a small, pitcher-like container. I was supposed to hold it under the sheet and go to the bathroom in it.

Something I didn't know. It is impossible to go to the bathroom in a small pitcher-like container while lying on your back while somebody is sewing up your arm and your nose itches.

The doctor finished my arm, and they put me in a wheelchair and took me to my room. I was finally able to relieve myself, drink a cold glass of tea, and fall into bed.

I spent the rest of the afternoon watching old movies

33

on the television above me and answering calls from wellwishers.

The doctor who had performed the cath came in after dinner.

"We'll look at the films together tomorrow," he said.

"I'd rather not, if you don't mind," I replied.

"You should look," he said.

I guess they teach that sort of thing in medical school—how to say a lot by saying very little.

* * * *

The films. They were in black and white. It cost nearly a thousand bucks to have cardiac catheterization. The least they could do, I was thinking to myself as I sat in my doctor's darkened office, was to put these flicks in color.

First, we looked at movies of a normal heart. I didn't like it when the doctor said that first, we were going to look at pictures of a "normal" heart.

The normal heart looks like an air bag. It fills with blood. Then, it collapses and becomes nearly flat, as it forces the blood out into the rest of the body.

Next, we looked at movies of my heart taken the day before.

It was big. It was fat. It labored. It looked like a stuffed grapefruit about to drown in its own juices.

"It can't go on like this indefinitely," the doctor said.

I could see that for myself now.

All the heart could do, said the doctor, was get

larger and larger. The heart muscle, said the doctor, was like a rubber band. Stretch it far enough and stretch it for a long time, and it will lose its elasticity, its ability to return to a normal size.

Surgery was no longer the question. The question was when to have surgery. My doctors conferred. Two schools of thought emerged:

DO THE SURGERY NOW. The patient is relatively young and otherwise healthy, an excellent surgical risk. Although there are no overt symptoms and the heart is doing its job now, deterioration of the patient's condition could come quickly. "Plus," said one of my doctors, "it's a good time of the year to have an operation."

"A good time of the year?"

"It's easier to recover in cool weather. It doesn't itch as much when your hair starts growing back."

They're going to shave my head to operate on my heart? More on this later.

HOLD OFF ON THE SURGERY. The patient's condition is not critical at this point. Put him on medication that will take some of the work load off the heart and watch him closely for the next few months and make a decision on the surgery later.

"We're not exactly talking about taking out your tonsils here," said one of my doctors. "You can die from heart surgery, you know."

On the other hand, it was a good time of year to die. Nobody roasts from the hot weather at the funeral.

I put the final (excuse the term) decision into the hands of the eldest of my doctors, a respected and

35

honored man with graying temples, who stands tall and erect and speaks softly, yet directly, the kind of man you want in the cockpit during a thunderstorm.

He looked at my cath films again. He studied my X-rays, and my EKG, and he listened to the sound of my heart.

He called me into his office and he sat me down on a couch in front of him.

"Now," he said.

"Now?"

"Now," he continued. "Do the surgery now. We are talking about replacing your aortic valve. We are talking about your heart returning to its normal size after the surgery, and we are talking about returning you to a normal life, and you should feel very fortunate about this."

"Fortunate?"

"Very fortunate," said the doctor. "Just twenty-five years ago, there was no such operation as this. We couldn't have even had this conversation because there would have been nothing we could have done for you."

"Now," the man had said. No more putting it off, no more thinking there might still be an escape hatch in this thing after all.

I was given a list of names of surgeons.

"They're all quite capable," I was told, "but the choice is up to you."

"Is it possible to spend a week living at each one's house?" I asked. "I'd like to get a little drift on their lifestyles."

This, of course, was out of the question.

"Then give me the one with the best won-loss record or anybody nicknamed 'Fingers'," I said.

I finally chose a surgeon.

"Great hands," they said of him.

"Personal habits?"

"Married. Kids."

"Won-loss?"

"Leads the league."

All that was necessary after that was to find a date both the surgeon and I could be available for our little appointment.

I checked my calendar.

"Anytime January '85 is fine with me," I said.

We compromised, and settled on two weeks from the following Wednesday.

III

The Hog and I

How the hog, one of God's most interesting creations, got involved in the surgery on my heart is a long story. After we had set a date for my appointment with the man with the knife, the doctors sat me down to discuss one remaining question.

We know we want to put in a new aortic valve in your heart, they said, but we don't know which type.

Which type? You mean this is like going into Baskin-Robbins and trying to decide between almond toffee and chocolate marshmallow? I wouldn't know an aortic valve if it walked up and bit me on the leg. What is this business with types?

I had a feeling when the discussion began that this little matter wouldn't be simple. It wasn't. I will attempt to decipher for you what the doctors attempted to explain to me.

In the first place, valve replacement isn't something that has been going on for years as my senior doctor had explained when I was trying to weasel my way out of having the operation in the first place.

Twenty-five years ago, the man had said, they would have put me on some pills and then we would have all sat around and waited for my heart to get the size of my head, which would have been about the time it would have stopped beating, a situation terribly hazardous to one's health.

Finally, somebody did invent an artificial heart valve and procedures whereby it could be inserted in place of the one the patient came with. The first valves were mechanical and were constructed of totally artificial materials, such as plastic.

They were better than no replacement valves at all, but there were problems. Patients with the mechanical valves faced the possibility of such complications as blood-clotting, which could lead to such unpleasant situations as strokes. So, it was necessary for patients with mechanical valves to take anti-coagulants to avoid the clotting, but thin blood isn't such a terrific idea, either. The biggest plus for mechanical valves was they were durable.

There obviously have been improvements in mechanical valves over the ensuing years, but the dangers of clotting and stroke and the matter of taking blood thinners indefinitely have remained.

"Little boogers will last just about forever," one of my doctors said, "but if we put one of those in you, I'd hate to see you dragging a foot around because of a stroke somewhere down the road."

I can understand doctors when they talk like that. Dragging a foot around isn't exactly my style.

Fortunately, I had another choice. A decade or so ago, researchers had the bright idea of attempting to develop a valve made from animal tissue. In the beginning, I suppose they tried taking valves from all sorts of animals and testing them for use in the human heart.

I would have started with elephants. When is the last time you've heard of an elephant dropping dead with a heart attack? I would have stayed away from nervous animals like those monkeys you see at the zoo who can't sit still and make those awful screeching noises.

I probably would have never thought of hogs. Hogs make all sorts of noises, too, like they're having trouble breathing; they don't get out of the mud or away from the food trough long enough to get any exercise; and then there is the matter of their smell.

When I was growing up in Coweta County, Georgia, a lot of people raised hogs. You could always tell which of your classmates had hogs at their house by noticing if there were empty seats around them in the classroom.

The Rainwaters raised hogs. Nobody would ever take a seat next to a Rainwater child in school because it was difficult to pay attention to what was the average per annum rainfall in Ethiopia and fight off the distinct odor of swine at the same time. Claude Rainwater, who was in my class, even had a pet hog, which he occasionally rode to school. The hog's name was Lamar. Claude would tie Lamar to a small tree in the school yard and Lamar would wait patiently until school was out and then Claude would ride him home again.

43

One day, Claude came to school without Lamar. He was in tears.

"What's the matter, Claude?" the teacher asked him.

"It's my pet hog," said Claude. "Daddy won't let me ride him to school anymore."

"Why is that?" the teacher continued.

"Daddy said he was going to have puppies."

Perhaps they should have told us less about the rainfall in Ethiopia in those days and spent at least a little time on why hogs don't have puppies, and even if one did, why it certainly shouldn't be named Lamar.

I was very surprised when my doctors told me my other choice for a new valve was one that would be taken from a hog. Only they didn't say "hog valve," they said "porcine valve," which is the same thing. Hog. Porcine. They both grunt and will eat things the dogs won't touch.

The advantage a valve taken from a hog would have over a mechanical valve, they explained, was the hog valve reduced the possibility of dangerous clotting and also required no blood thinners. Hog valves and human valves, they said, were very much alike.

I waited for the catch. The catch, they said, was the question of the durability of the animal tissue valve.

"It won't last as long as a mechanical valve?" I asked.

"How many fifty-year-old hogs do you know?" was the answer.

Specifically, the porcine valves have been in use for something like ten years, and those implanted in the beginning have exhibited a tendency to wear out.

"What happens if one wears out?" I asked further.

"A second operation for a new one."

I did some quick arithmetic. I'm thirty-five. I plan to live out my years. I'll take seventy-five and call it even.

At one operation to put in a new valve every ten years, that's four operations to go. At that rate, I could wipe out a small hog farm like the Rainwaters' by myself.

Plus, there was the consideration of something out of a hog being placed inside my body. I mentioned some of the things that worried me about hogs, their snorting and labored breathing, their diet, their acute laziness, and their smell.

Despite all that, however, I have always had a voracious appetite for barbecue and even fancy myself as quite the expert on the subject. What would happen to me with hog in my heart?

Every time I'd pass a barbecue restaurant, my eyes would fill with tears?

Barbecue. My thoughts raced back to the integral part it has played in my life.

There was the annual Fourth of July Barbecue in my hometown. The churches went in together and bought some hogs and then the menfolk would sit up all night before the Fourth and barbecue the hogs over hickory smoke in an open pit, which doesn't take a great deal of work once the hogs are cooking, so the menfolk had a lot of time to sit around and talk, mostly about the Bible.

They would talk Revelation for a time, which always spooked me, and then they would get along to something like Deuteronomy.

The Fourth of July Barbecue drew people from as

45

far away as Newnan, LaGrange, and Hogansville. One year, a man from North Carolina was passing through and stopped in to partake.

He asked for cole slaw.

"What for?" somebody asked. "There's plenty of stew and light bread."

"I want to put it on my barbecue," the man from North Carolina said.

I learned my first rule about barbecue that day. You don't put cole slaw on it. I think that's in Deuteronomy somewhere.

Somebody pulled a knife on the man and he got back in his car and went back to North Carolina.

After I left home, I roamed freely about other parts of the country, and I came to understand several truths about barbecue:

—The best barbecue is served in the state of Georgia. In Texas, they barbecue beef, which isn't barbecue at all, and neither is goat, which is stringy. I wouldn't even put cole slaw on barbecued goat out of respect for the cole slaw.

—The best barbecue is found in family-run operations. Harold Hembree, who runs Harold's Barbecue in Atlanta, can't even count the number of cousins and nieces and nephews working for him. There are three generations of Sprayberrys cooking and serving at Sprayberry's in Newnan, Georgia. Sweat's is a family operation in Soperton, Georgia, and it was Jim Brewer's father-in-law who first started Fresh-Air in Jackson, Georgia, fifty-one years ago when he served off a sawdust floor. "When it's a family working together," says Jim Brewer, "things get done right."

—If there are religious posters on the wall, you can usually count on the barbecue's being good. Harold's is a perfect example.

—Good barbecue restaurants rarely serve beer, as good as beer is with barbecue. "Mama won't allow it here," is why Harold Hembree doesn't serve beer at his place. "You'll lose your family trade," says Jim Brewer of Fresh-Air.

—If a restaurant specializes in something besides barbecue, the barbecue probably won't be any good. You can serve other things, just don't brag on it. Jack Sweat in Soperton is still amazed at the time a family of Yankees headed for Florida stopped by his place and ordered fried shrimp.

—Georgia barbecue restaurants are careful what kind of bread they serve with their meat. Normally, it's thin buns for sandwiches, and white bread for plates. Harold's toasts white bread over an open flame for sandwiches and serves cracklin' cornbread with its plates. I think Harold will go to heaven for his cracklin' cornbread.

—Brunswick stew is too complicated to get into. Everybody has a different idea about how it should be cooked and what it should contain. "We even get 'em who complain unless the stew's been cooked in a hog's head," says Jim Brewer.

—Sauce: Ditto. In Georgia alone there are hundreds of varieties of sauces. If the meat is good, the sauce will be, too.

—It is important to put up a sign in a barbecue restaurant that says "No Shoes. No Shirt. No Service." That will add class to the place by keeping out people from Texas and North Carolina.

My doctors assured me the installation of a porcine valve into my heart would have no effect upon my taste and desire and enjoyment for good barbecue.

"You might have some other problems, though," said one.

"What's that?" I asked.

"You might want to go out and root for truffles occasionally," he laughed.

"And you might crave watermelon rinds and corn-cobs," said another.

"What you really have to watch," a third chimed in, "is every afternoon about four o'clock, you might get this strange desire to go out and make love in the mud."

Doctors stay inside too much, I think.

Aside from the questions of the durability of the valves and the barbecue thing, there were a couple of other concerns.

I wondered where they kept the hogs who were kind enough to donate their valves for people in my condition.

You know the outrage we have over the slaughter of baby seals. They go out and hit those baby seals in the head with a lead pipe or something, and people are up in the air about that everywhere.

I was afraid they kept the hogs in a pen out behind the hospital. I've been prepared for surgery and the doctor says to an orderly, "Leon, go out to the hog pen and get me a valve."

Leon goes out to the hog pen with a two-by-four and whomps a hog on the head and they take out his valve.

The doctors assured me nothing like that took place, which was a relief. Hogs have feelings, too, I expect.

I considered the question of porcine versus mechanical valve for about a minute.

MECHANICAL: I couldn't get the idea of dragging a leg very far out of my mind.

PORCINE: So it wears out in ten years. At least I wouldn't have to take the blood thinners and worry about a stroke. And medical science moves so swiftly. In ten years, who knows? Maybe they would come up with a solution where you just take a pill.

There was just that one other thing I wanted to know after the decision was made to install the porcine valve.

"It's just a little thing," I said.

"Shoot," said one of the doctors.

"Do the pigs that give up their valves have names?" The doctor said he would check.

"Do you have a preference of a name for your donor?" he asked.

"Not really," I answered. "Just as long as it isn't Lamar."

IV

An Awful Attack of Sentimentality

I SPENT a lot of time during those last couple of weeks before my surgery taking stock of my life, which currently amounted to thirty-five years and some change. Thirty-five.

When I was ten, I had wanted to be sixteen, so I could drive a car. When I was sixteen, I had wanted to be twenty-one so I could walk into a bar and order a drink. When I was twenty-one, I had wanted to be thirty, so I could pontificate on the great issues of the day and nobody would say, "What on earth is that kid talking about?"

When I was thirty, I was satisfied. I think thirty is the perfect age. At thirty, you can do all the things grownups do, like invest in a tax shelter or smoke a cigar, but you're still young enough to waste your money on sports cars.

But thirty-five. It's a strange age. The primary danger at thirty-five is there is a tendency to commit the grievous error of allowing the mind to write a check the body can't cash, to quote an unnamed philosopher.

Drinking. At thirty-five, you begin to find out all the bad things that are supposed to happen to you if you drink too much certainly will.

Sex. Thirty-five is the first time you realize you can go six months without it and it won't kill you.

Money. Thirty-five is when you realize even if it did grow on trees, somebody else would probably own all the trees.

Ambition. By the time you're thirty-five you are about ready to settle for what you can get.

At thirty-five, I'd had three wives. We've been over that already. At thirty-five, I'd also had twice that many jobs and some fine dogs.

The best dog I'd ever owned was a bassett hound named "Plato." Basset hounds are wonderful dogs. If you feel bad, they always look like they feel worse.

To be perfectly honest, I've always gotten along better with dogs than with women. Dogs don't seem to want as much. Come home in the middle of the night and a dog won't ask you where you've been or how much money you've spent or why you hadn't called.

A dog is satisfied with the fact you're there at all.

I lost my basset hound Plato to my first wife in a custody battle. She took him to live with her and the next I heard of him, he had died. But the dog had class to the end.

"He came down with cancer in his old age," my first wife wrote me. "One morning, he went to the refrigerator and began to beg for food. I gave him a raw hot dog. He took it out to a little creek behind the house where he liked to play. It was a hot day. He sprawled out in the cool water, finished off the hot dog, and died."

Class.

I didn't sleep much those last two weeks. It seemed like a waste of time somehow. I still shook the bed. My wife was a trooper. She endured the bed shaking. She endured the restlessness. She endured the awful attack of sentimentality that struck me. The future seemed at least slightly suspect at the time, so I dealt mostly with the past.

My past. Thirty-five years of it. Wives and dogs. A career. Family. My mother. She's been ill for so long herself. Something called scleroderma. It attacked her esophagus. She taught first grade nearly thirty years before the illness forced her retirement. That long with first graders is enough to make anybody sick, I suppose.

When I told my mother, who had only one child, I would be having heart surgery, she said to make sure my underwear was clean when I went to the hospital.

Mothers. Their love is the best love.

The first grade students called my mother, their teacher, "Miss Christine." I called her, and still do, "Mama." She began teaching in my school, Moreland Elementary in Moreland, Georgia, when I was in the second grade, and if your mother happens to be on the faculty of your school, it is difficult for you because the other students think you get special treatment, and if you do anything wrong, your teachers will say to you, "Your mother taught you better than this," because they presume a teacher's child has been taught better than to flush a cherry bomb down a school commode just to hear the marvelous, thunderous sound the subsequent explosion will make.

Sammy Whitten and I once flushed a cherry bomb down each of the four commodes in the boys' restroom of Moreland School. I ran. He stayed to see the water explode out of the commodes. Sammy Whitten was captured by school authorities at the scene. I am forever indebted to him for not fingering his accomplice. All he ever asked in return was half my lunch the next five years we were in school together.

The school drew children from the town of Moreland which was no town at all. We got other children, too, from out in the county. Sawmill kids. Pulpwood cutter kids. Sheet rocker kids. Sharecropper kids. Kids with no shoes. Kids in tattered overalls. Kids on free lunches.

It was at this point in my life that I noticed poverty for the first time. The term, in those days, for poor people was "white trash." Real bad white trash was "lowdown white trash" and white trash even worse than that was "sorry white trash." Sorry white trash lived in whatever it could find, like dogs, and ate from garbage cans and slept five and six to a bed and married their first cousins and all traveled in a broken down car and didn't bathe.

Some sorry white trash moved on the outside of town when I was about to enter the fifth grade. Their name was Hadley. There was an old man and an old woman. They looked like the last time they saw soap, it was heading in the other direction. They had a mess of children around them, too—four, five, or six of them.

Some were their kids, some were their grandchildren whose parents had run off. The old man drove an old rattletrap, of course, and it sunk low in the back and burned oil and the stuffings and the springs were coming out of the seat covers.

My friend Danny Thompson and I walked down near the Hadley house one day because Danny, who had seen "lowdown white trash" had never really seen any "sorry white trash." But the dogs got after us before we could get too close.

White trash, no matter what level, always attracted dogs. Yard dogs. Dogs that liked to crawl under trucks on hot days and get oil all over their backs. One way to distinguish a yard dog from a regular dog: Call a regular dog and he'll come at you nose first with at least some degree of enthusiasm. Yard dogs come with a sideways gait, backing and shying, in case there's a boot to dodge when they get there.

The year was 1956. Don Larsen pitched his perfect game that year. Luckily for us, Danny Thompson and I thought, there were no Hadleys joining us in the fifth grade.

"Any new students in your class?" my mother asked me at supper the night after the first day of classes.

"Few, but none of those sorry, white trash Hadleys," I said.

My mother, incidentally, was not aware of the categorizations of white trash, nor of white trash at all, for that matter.

She made me leave the kitchen without my dinner

57

and I was told never to refer to anyone as "sorry" or "trash" again. Then, she did something even worse to me.

"When I go to the Hadley's," my mother said, "you're going with me."

Mama did have a Hadley in her class in the first grade. His name was Sammy, she said. He was blond and he had blue eyes. He didn't talk much, she said, but when she had sent him home for the day, he had, without a word, hugged her around the neck. And, Mama had to visit the Hadleys because school regulations required that each teacher visit the home of each child in her class, in order to meet the parents and get a firsthand view of the homelife.

I offered Danny Thompson the half of my lunch Sammy Whitten wasn't getting to go along with me, but he said he heard those people carried bad diseases and he didn't want to catch one.

When Mama and I drove up to the Hadleys, the dogs came down off the porch where they had been sitting with the children on the car seat, the one with the stuffings and the springs coming out. The little brown dog yapped some, but he was too small to be of any threat, and the two big dogs had a lot of mileage on them. They had come down out of natural yard dog hospitality.

Four children—one, a toddler in last week's diapers; another, a couple of years older; another, maybe five, with lots of sores on his hands and face; and then a smiling, blue-eyed child of six, he would be Sammy, continued to stare at us from the porch.

"Hi, Sammy," said my mother. "These your brothers and sisters?" Sammy nodded, yes.

Two older children than appeared in the front door. One was a girl, twelve maybe; the other, a boy, her older brother. He could have been fifteen. According to the boy, they were aunt and uncle to the younger children whose mother, their sister, had split with a truck driver three months earlier and "didn't have no head for ever comin' back."

Mr. Hadley emerged. Even his hands were angry hands. I moved closer to my mother.

"I'm Miss Christine, Mr. Hadley," said my mother. I marveled at the way she spoke straight at him, politely, like he was a preacher and not, as I thought to myself, sorry white trash.

"I'm Sammy's teacher," she went on, "and it is the policy of the school that I visit with you and tell you of Sammy's progress and attitude in the classroom."

I knew my mother would have the good sense to discuss all this on the front porch and not move inside that awful house.

"Could we go inside to discuss this, Mr. Hadley?" asked my mother.

Mr. Hadley, with one shake of his giant, hairy, dirty, angry hand, motioned us inside.

More automobile seats from a raid on a junkyard. Crates. Tables with a leg missing. Lanterns. Fireplace. Feed company calendar on the wall—the only decoration. July showing in the shank of September.

There are sounds of movement in another room, the

59

kitchen perhaps. Must be Mrs. Hadley. She emerges. Ma Kettle after fighting a forest fire all night.

My mother rises. "Mrs. Hadley?" my mother greets her.

The woman nods and defers to her husband.

"You want to talk about Sammy?" he asks.

"You're his father, Mr. Hadley?"

"Grandpaw. His maw run off. She wasn't no count and she run off. Don't know who his paw was. Could'a been any one of a bunch of 'em."

"Your occupation, Mr. Hadley?"

"Sawmill hand."

It is at this point I notice Mr. Hadley has no teeth. I check Mrs. Hadley. She has no teeth, either. Older boy's and older girl's teeth appear to be in serious jeopardy, too.

Sammy, the one with the blond hair and the blue eyes, is still outside, but he is half-peering through the open door. He senses the conversation has to do with him.

My mother is handling this well. The place smells of burning tires. My mother sits there quietly asking questions about the Hadley family's medical history.

"Heart disease?"

"No."

"Mental disorders?"

"Had a cousin went crazy once. He got run over by a train."

"Diabetes?"

"Don't let my kids get close enough to no bad dogs to get no diabetes."

"You're thinking about rabies, Mr. Hadley."

"Diabeetees, raybeetees, don't want these kids gettin' bit by no bad dogs."

Undaunted, my mother moves on.

"Sammy, I'm sure you will like to know, is very cooperative at school. He seems to be able to concentrate for long periods, and I think that will be very beneficial to him."

I can see Sammy inch his face a little farther into the open door. My mother is continuing to talk to Mr. and Mrs. Hadley. Mrs. Hadley, I get the impression, last spoke in the late thirties and, probably, was reprimanded for that.

"The only problem with him seems to be that I can't get him to open up and talk. I'd like for him to be more verbal in the classroom. Do you notice his lack of participation in conversation at home?"

Mr. Hadley has had enough.

"Teacherlady," he begins. "I ain't never been to no school myself. Ain't had time, trying to raise all these young'uns. My wife can read and write well enough to get both us by. All I know is if you want Sammy to talk, you do what I do. You beat it out of him."

With that, Mr. Hadley reaches over the fireplace and produces a leather strap bound to a crude wooden handle.

"You take this here with you to school, teacherlady. You want him to shut his mouth, you pop his butt with this strap. You want one to open his mouth, you do the same. That's what I made this here thing for. Children ought to be whooped if they don't mind.

61

"Sammy, come here!" Mr. Hadley beckons the youngster peering from the door. The child comes quickly.

"Show the teacherlady what happened to you last week when I asked you a question and you wouldn't answer it."

Sammy, embarrassed but obedient, pulls off his tattered shirt, revealing the welts of a beating.

My mother is very calm.

"I don't think I need such a thing to convince my students to talk or to be quiet, Mr. Hadley," she says sternly. I would have given up my after-school candy money for the rest of my educational career to have at that moment seen my mama take that strap to Mr. Hadley.

My mother excused herself, thanked the Hadleys for their time, and said to Sammy as she left, "I'll see you at school tomorrow."

Sammy smiled timidly.

We were back in our car. The dogs had left us and had gone back to the porch. I was first to see him coming.

"It's Sammy, Mama," I said.

He was running, his blond bangs falling over his face, over his blue eyes. He came to the door on the driver's side, and my mother opened it for him.

He never said a word to either of us. He just stood there, looking up at my mother, begging her, craving her, needing her.

Then, he jumped into her arms, into our car, into her lap, and his arms locked tightly around her neck and

62

he squeezed her and then as quickly as he had come, he was gone again, trotting back up the stairs to the rotting porch and into the rotting house.

My mother didn't cry then. But I heard her crying later. In the night, she cried because she still felt those little arms tight around her neck and still saw those welts on Sammy's back.

One day Sammy wasn't at school anymore and there was no trace of him at any other county school, and my mother even went so far as to check state records, but she found no trace of the Hadley's whereabouts.

It was a year or so later. We were deep into the Georgia winter and my mother sat in our living room, staring out the front window into a howling, cold night. We had eggs and grits and homemade biscuits with sorghum syrup for supper. My mother always cooked eggs and grits and biscuits on cold nights.

She continued to stare into the dark.

"I wonder if little Sammy is warm right now," she said, suddenly.

Later, in the deep secret of her night, she cried again for little Sammy.

* * * *

My daddy. He died when I was twenty-three, when he was fifty-eight. I spent a lot of time in those weeks before surgery looking at a picture of him I keep on my desk in my basement. He is wearing the uniform of the United States Army.

I never really knew the man. He came back from World War II and married my mother. In 1946, they did their part for the war baby boom. We moved around a lot those first years, and then Korea broke out and my father went back to war.

"The first time I went," I can remember him saying, "I was young and it was a great adventure. When I went back the second time, I already knew about the hell I was getting into."

One man, two wars. He was an infantryman, and he was a fine soldier. I still have the Bronze Star, the citation for his battlefield commission, the Purple Hearts. Years after his death, I ran into a war buddy of his.

"Your daddy was as brave a man as I ever met," he said. "He was good with the kids, the nineteen-year-olds who went in first. He led them through France. He knew the odds against him. Every night, we would talk and every night he would say, 'I know I'm going to die tomorrow.' He drank up France—trying to get that thought off his mind."

Six years after surviving France he was commanding a rifle company in Korea. He told the story often. I remember every word:

"We were near a rice paddy, about to move out. Suddenly, the rice paddy started shooting at us. There were gooks everywhere.

"The Germans were easier to fight than these people. You could figure out what a German would do. In many ways, he was like an American. He feared death. Not the gooks. They would come in waves. You kill a thousand, another thousand would be there to take their place.

"It was nearly dark. They turned spotlights on us. They blew horns and whistles and shot off firecrackers and they screamed, and they kept coming and they kept coming.

"We fought through the night. They were tearing us apart. We managed to dig a small trench. Maybe twenty of us were left. At daybreak, a mortar barrage hit directly in the trench. It took a kid's head clean off. The head rolled away from the kid's body.

"I will never forget looking at that face. It smiled. I swear that face had a smile on it. The chaplain was still alive. He looked up at me and said, 'Captain, you have just seen a man go to heaven.' "

More mortars came flying in. There was more death. The gooks overran the camp.

"I was still in the trench," my father would go on, his listeners enthralled. I don't know how much was embellishment. Very little, I suppose. Combat usually leaves little to the imagination.

"I was cut and I was bleeding, but I was alive. I figured they would find me still breathing and shoot me. I resigned myself to it. I wondered if my body would ever get back home. When we buried my mama, there was a place near her. I remember looking at that place and thinking that's where I'd like to go when my own time came.

"I crawled near two dead bodies that were lying close to each other. I put my head face down with my nose in my helmet. I didn't want them to see my breath move the dirt in the trench.

"I heard rounds being fired. They were shooting the wounded, the bastards. Two gooks jumped into the trench. They began kicking bodies. They kicked the two bodies next to me, but they never kicked me. I don't know why. I was praying. I said, 'God, if they kick me, don't let me move, don't let me make a sound.'

"The gooks never touched me. They left me with the dead. I didn't move, even after I was positive they had left. When I finally crawled out of the trench, I couldn't believe I had been spared. We'd been wiped out. I found one other soldier, another kid, who was alive. But he had been wounded. I picked him up and started walking with him in my arms. I had no idea where I was going. I just walked. When I got so tired I couldn't walk any longer, I sat the kid down and leaned him against a tree. He was unconscious. I leaned against the tree, myself, and went to sleep. When I woke up, it was dark again and the kid was dead."

So he wandered, stunned and alone.

"At daybreak, I came over a hill. I spotted a Korean boy standing a few yards in front of me. He had a grenade in his hands. I don't know where he got it, probably off a dead soldier. I scared him, I guess. He pulled the pin on the grenade and threw it at me. I hit the ground. I felt the explosion and I took shrapnel in the back of my head and in my neck. I blacked out.

"When I woke up, I was in some sort of lean-to. The Korean boy was wiping the blood off my face and neck.

He was South Korean and hadn't realized I was an American. That's all I could figure had happened. That's twice I should have been dead in a day. And some people say there's no God."

He hid in the lean-to for six weeks. A Papa-san, an old Korean man, maybe the boy's grandfather, brought him water and cold rice. Occasionally, he could hear enemy troops walking and talking near the lean-to. He dared not come out, not even to relieve himself.

It was dreadfully cold. His feet were frostbitten.

When the Korean boy thought it was safe, he led my father back to the American lines.

"I would have run back," he said, "but my feet were so swollen, it was like walking on two basketballs."

I remember the day the telegram came that said my father was missing in action. My mother cried. She tried to explain to me. I was five, so I cried, too. I didn't know exactly why I was crying, but when my mother pulled me to her, I wanted to share every inch of her grief.

Later, the word came that my father was alive. He called soon afterwards from a hospital in Pearl Harbor. My mother and I cried again. When he stepped off the train at Union Station in Atlanta, we met him with boxes of fried chicken and cathead country biscuits, and I sat in his lap and he squeezed me and that night, that incredible night, he came to the bed where I was sleeping and he picked me up and he took me to his bed and he put me down between himself and my mother and they reached their arms over me to each other. There has been no such peace and security in my soul since.

67

I don't know what happened to the man. Everybody who knew him had a theory. He couldn't sleep. He would come again to me at nights, and pick me up and hold me and I would rub the back of his head and feel the tiny bits of metal still lodged there from the Korean boy's grenade.

And he drank. First, it was nightly cocktails at the Officer's Club, but it graduated to benders. He had tried to drink up France. Now he was taking a shot at Fort Benning, Georgia.

The Army forsook him. They called him unfit. I think back to his feet. They bled so badly after he came home from Korea. Every night, he took off blood-soaked socks. And they called him unfit.

He took to the road. This job, that job. The man had talent. Big voice. Military bearing. Played the piano. Name it, he could charm it. Name a bank, and he could cash a check on it, which is why the road beckoned so often.

My mother divorced him. She had no choice. I was seven. I saw him a couple of times a year after that. He could always make me laugh.

They called me one morning from the hospital in the little town of Claxton, Georgia. He had collapsed on the street. I drove five hours from Atlanta. He was already in a coma when I got there.

I had never seen anybody die before. It wasn't like in the movies. He was in a deep sleep, and he took a breath, and then he didn't take another one. A nurse came into the hospital room and checked for his pulse and said there wasn't any. She called in a doctor who verified the lack of a pulse. My father's face was very blue. I held his hand and cried. I let his hand go when the doctor pulled the sheet over his head.

They said he died of respiratory failure due to pneumonia. No, he didn't. He died from the effects fighting two wars can have on a man.

Those nights before my surgery that I sat alone with his picture, I took on my fear, the fear of the pain that was ahead of me, the fear of death, and of something else that was even a worse fear, somehow.

Brand it macho, if you will, but I was thirty-five years old and I had carried around a burden or two, but there had been no real test of my courage, no challenge that had come close to this.

As I faced my first, gut-wrenching moment of truth, I was afraid I wouldn't take it like a man.

The picture helped. My own father. He led men into battle. He faked death out of its shorts too many times to count, and then he fought the booze and bad dreams and he didn't give up until something you can't find without a microscope felled him from the blind side.

If he could do all that, I assured myself, then I could do this.

A couple of days before I checked into the hospital, I drove out to the little cemetery where my father is buried, which is all I could do with the urge to thank him.

I'd never been so grateful that we had decided to put him in the place next to his mama.

V

Where Are You, Now That I Need You, Lucille?

I DIDN'T KNOW if it was okay to drink beer the night before you check into the hospital to have heart surgery, so I started calling doctors to find out. There were at least a half dozen involved in my case in one fashion or another.

The first doctor I reached said I probably shouldn't drink any beer the night before checking into the hospital.

"You don't want to show up with a hangover," he said.

I certainly don't think it would have been appropriate for any of my doctors to show up at the hospital the day of my surgery with a hangover, but I didn't see why it would be a problem for me to appear in that condition, so I continued calling doctors.

The third one I reached said, "Sure, you can have a beer."

A beer.

"Nobody drinks just one beer," I explained. "That's why they come in six-packs."

"Okay," said the doctor, "two beers."

"Draught okay?" I forged onward.

"Draught is fine," he said.

There is a store near my house that sells draught beer in gallon containers. I stuck to my doctor's orders and bought only two containers.

Beer has gotten me through a lot of tough spots in my life, and I will always be indebted to Ronnie Jenkins—you will recall him as the hero of Chapter I who taught me about women. He also taught me to drink beer.

My first lessons began at Lucille's beer joint in Grantville, Georgia. We were both fifteen. Old enough to buy it, old enough to drink it was Lucille's motto. Only we never actually bought any beer at Lucille's because we always made certain we drank with Mr. Hugh Frank Logan, a local farmer.

Mr. Hugh Frank was a large man, who toiled in his fields and enjoyed topping off the day with a few cool cans of Pabst Blue Ribbon, which is all Lucille served, except for Carling Black Label and nobody would drink that, not even Ronnie and I.

The problem with Mr. Hugh Frank was he was hard of hearing, so he talked in a very loud voice:

"LUCILLE," Mr. Hugh Frank would begin. "GIMME ONE UH THEM BLUE RIBBONS."

Because he was hard of hearing and talked in a loud voice, nobody wanted to stand around with Mr. Hugh Frank and drink beer. Except Ronnie.

"Watch this," he said to me one night after Mr. Hugh Frank had ordered his beer.

"HIYOUDOIN', MR. HUGH FRANK!" screamed Ronnie.

"NOT TODAY, BUT WE MIGHT GET A SHOWER TOMORROW," Mr. Hugh Frank replied.

"MRS. LOGAN DOING OKAY THESE DAYS, MR. HUGH FRANK?" Ronnie pressed on, a decibel or two louder.

"GOT ABOUT TWO MORE ACRES TO GO AND THEN I GOT TO HELP HARLEY BOTTS MOW HIS," Mr. Hugh Frank answered.

The fact he had misunderstood what Ronnie had asked had nothing to do with anything. The fact somebody—anybody—would attempt to talk to him brought out all sorts of generosity in Mr. Hugh Frank.

"LUCILLE," I can still hear him boom across the crowded room, over Ernest Tubb or Kitty Wells on the juke box, "GIMME 'NOTHER BLUE RIBBON. AND GIVE THESE HERE BOYS ONE, TOO."

Later in the evening, Ronnie would ask Mr. Hugh Frank his opinion of the Monroe Doctrine and Mr. Hugh Frank would buy us more beer.

* * * *

I had a terrible hangover when I awakened the morning I was to check into the hospital.

"The doctor told you not to drink a lot of beer," said my wife.

I should have married Lucille, I said to myself.

75

I packed a little bag. I put in my toothbrush, shaving cream and razor, bedroom slippers, and some aspirin for my hangover.

"They'll give you aspirin at the hospital," said my wife.

"These are for the drive over there," I said.

"Did you remember to take pajamas?" my wife continued.

I don't wear pajamas. I am firmly convinced a man who wears pajamas also drinks whiskey sours and then eats those silly little cherries that come with the drink.

"Here are the pajamas I gave you for Christmas," my wife went on. "Nobody goes to the hospital without pajamas."

I asked my wife to describe the medical journal in which she had picked up that piece of information. She said if I didn't take pajamas the doctors and nurses would know I slept in my underwear. I asked what was wrong with the doctors and nurses knowing that I slept in my underwear. She said men who sleep in their underwear sit up half the night drinking beer and then they belch and snore.

That wouldn't have bothered Lucille, I said to myself.

I was told to be at the hospital at 10:30 in the morning. I took my little bag with my toilet articles, bedroom slippers, and pajamas inside, and I walked out of my house and into my garage. I sat down in my car, turned on the engine and backed the car out into the driveway.

76

As I was about to pull away, my wife came out to my car and said, "If you don't want to take the pajamas, don't take them. I'm sorry I made such an issue about it."

"You know something," I said to her. "If you owned a beer joint, you'd be perfect."

* * * *

I chose to have my operation at Emory University Hospital in Atlanta for two reasons: It has an excellent reputation as one of the world's leading centers for heart surgery, and the Atlanta transit system runs buses that pass directly in front of the hospital.

A nice nurse showed me to my room. It reminded me of the dormitory room I had when I was a freshman in college, not exactly the Ramada Inn, but better than the accommodations at the Laredo Correctional Institute.

The first thing I did after the nurse left was to check the lone window in my room. It wasn't locked. The next thing I did was check to see how far away was the ground. Three stories. Tie a few bedsheets together and I could be out of here and on a bus in a matter of minutes. You plan ahead at a time like this.

I soon learned why they insist you be checked into the hospital nearly twenty-four hours before your surgery—so every doctor and nurse on the lot, and the guy mopping the hall, if he is so inclined, can ask you a lot of questions.

I hadn't been in my room fifteen minutes when a

doctor wearing a beard and some rather strange shoes that looked like ballet slippers came in with a clipboard and began discussing my medical history with me.

"Diabetes?"

"No."

"Blurred vision?"

"You mean when I'm sober?"

"Yes."

"No."

"Ulcers?"

"No."

"Asthma?"

"No."

"Bronchitis?"

"No."

"Venereal disease?"

"What kind of question is that?"

"Just answer it."

"No."

"Kidney failure?"

"No."

"Pneumonia?"

"No."

"Hemophilia?"

"Do what?"

"Is there any history of hemophilia in your family?"

"Third cousin on my mother's side."

"He was a hemophiliac?"

"Well, we weren't certain, but he wore ballet slippers to work."

78

"Is there anything you need?"

"Aspirin."

Later, the anesthesiologist came into my room and asked me more questions.

"Have you ever been put to sleep before?" she inquired.

"You mean outside a truck stop?"

Soon, it was time for lunch. If you have ever been in a hospital, you know about the kind of food they have there.

For lunch, I received some Jello, English peas, and something served in chunks with brown, lumpy gravy poured on top of it.

I hate Jello. Jello isn't food at all. Children like Jello because they can see themselves in it and it jiggles when you put a fork in it. I don't eat anything that jiggles.

I hate English peas, too. Once I went to Boy Scout camp and they served English peas every night for dinner. One evening, I made the mistake of indicating how much I disliked English peas.

"Young man," said my Scout leader, "there are children all over China starving, and yet you turn up your nose at these peas."

"I would like to take the first step toward helping solve the world food shortage problem by donating my English peas to the starving children of China," I said.

Boy Scout leaders seldom have good senses of humor. He made me eat all my English peas and all that were left in the bowl before I could go back to my cabin and shoot craps with the other campers.

I vowed that night never to eat another English pea. I hope the starving children in China appreciate my gesture.

The chunky substance with the lumpy gravy on it. I asked the woman who brought it into my room if she knew what it was.

"Looks like some kind of stew," she said.

"Stewed what?" I asked.

"I don't cook it, I just serve it," she answered.

I stuck my fork in it. It jiggled a couple of times and then hopped out of my plate and ran under the bed. I suppose they have to do something with those laboratory animals after they are through experimenting with them.

After lunch, they showed me a slide show concerning what to expect after I was finished with my surgery. This was when I first learned about the tubes they were going to put in my body.

The slides pictured a male patient in the Intensive Care Unit following his surgery. I looked at all the tubes that were running in and out of him and I noticed he was smiling and seemed to be in no discomfort whatsoever.

You can't put that many tubes in a man and manage to keep a smile on his face. Either the man was simply an actor playing the part of a patient, I surmised, or he was dead. I know what probably killed him, too. He ate the chunky stuff with the lumpy brown gravy on it.

They ran all sorts of tests on me. A nurse came in and took out something sharp and cut a slice out of my arm.

"Okay, I'll eat the food," I said.

She explained I wasn't being punished. She was merely checking to see how I bled.

I bled pretty well. All down my arm, in fact.

"That's perfect," the nurse said smiling, while I laid there bleeding all down my arm.

"There's a knife fight Saturday night," I said to the nurse. "Want to go?"

I think she would have cut me on the other arm, but a doctor walked in to check my heart. He put his stethoscope to my chest and then he asked if I wanted to take a listen.

I had never heard my own heart beat. I asked what to listen for.

"The sound the heart is supposed to make goes like this: 'lub-dub, lub-dub, lub-dub,' " the doctor said. "If you will listen closely, you will hear yours go, 'lub-dub, shhhh, lub-dub, shhhh, lub-dub, shhhh.' The shhhh is the sound of the blood leaking back through your valve."

I listened. The doctor was wrong. My heart didn't go "lub-dub, shhh." It went "lub-dub-dub-dub-dub, bzzzt."

"The only way your heart would be making a sound like that is if you had sat up half last night and drank two gallons of beer," the doctor said.

My surgeon peeked in. I could tell from his voice he had a slight cold.

"Try not to worry about a thing," he said, just before he sneezed.

As soon as he left, I called for the guy with the weird shoes and asked for Valium, as much as they could spare.

Nobody had mentioned the shave to me. There was a knock on my door.

"Come in," I said. More questions or more tests.

A man entered carrying a pan of water.

"I'm Doctor Prep," he said, pulling a razor out of the pan of water.

"Doctor Prep?"

"I'm the one who preps you for surgery," he said.

"Preps me?"

"Shaves you."

"I shaved this morning."

"Not where I'm going to shave you."

I looked at the window. If I couldn't get out through there, I thought, maybe I could hide under the bed with my lunch.

Escape was out of the question. I pulled back the covers.

"Nice pajamas," said Doctor Prep.

"Say that without that razor in your hand," I said back to him.

I took off my pajamas. I was wearing nothing but my hair. In thirty-five years, I had accumulated quite a bit of hair on my body. Hair can cause infections during surgery.

Dr. Prep took most of it. He started at my neck. He shaved my chest. He shaved my stomach. He spent ten minutes shaving in my navel. I didn't even know I had hair in my navel.

He shaved on. When he got to my dignity, I closed my eyes.

He stopped at my knees.

"When we do bypass," he said, "I shave 'em all the way down to their ankles."

In bypass heart surgery, they take portions of arteries from the legs to replace the clogged arteries near the heart.

"You seem to enjoy this work," I said to Dr. Prep.

"Beats plucking chickens," he answered, closing the door behind him.

I figured the worst was over. Then, there was another knock on the door.

I wasn't going to be surprised again.

"Who is it?" I said.

"Come to check your plumbing," a voice answered.

That's all I needed. I'd been questioned and re-questioned, had a nurse cut my arm and a man shave my knees, legs, chest, privates, and belly bald and now here came the man with the rubber glove.

I couldn't bear to look. I rolled over on my stomach, beckoned him in, and waited for the intrusion. Thirty seconds later, I heard the toilet in my restroom flush. I turned around and there stood a man wearing a brown shirt with his name sewn over the pocket holding a plunger.

"Nothing to worry about now," he said. "It flushes fine."

I called for more Valium.

There were only a couple of more things. There was the enema. I will spare you the details of that. I was told I could order something out to eat if I didn't want what the

83

hospital was serving for dinner. I think they were afraid maybe I had a gun and would use it if they brought me anything else to eat out of the hospital kitchen.

I sent my wife out for chili dogs. I saved them until after my enema. A hospital patient takes his revenge where he can.

Night came. Twelve hours to go. The nurse slipped her head through the door and said I had a visitor.

"If he doesn't have a razor, let him in," I said.

My minister walked into my room.

"Anything on your mind?" he asked.

"Pull up a chair," I answered.

VI

Good Men of God

B ROTHER DAVE GARDNER, the southern philosopher, used to talk about how his mother had wanted him to be a man of God.

"My mother used to say, 'Son, you could make a million dollars preaching,' " he would begin. "I'd say, 'Yeah, Mama, but what the hell would I spend it on?' "

It's not easy being a preacher, especially these days. Preachers have to work harder than ever before keeping their flocks in line what with temptations at a new all-time high. I suppose the really big-time preachers, like Billy Graham and Oral Roberts and Jerry Falwell, have it made, though. Every time I pick up a newspaper there's a story about one of those heavyweight television preachers making a trip to Russia, or speaking out on international issues, or having a vision that tells him to go out and raise a few million bucks.

I always wonder when those guys find time to work on their sermons. When do they visit the sick and marry people and preach funerals?

Who mows the grass around their churches, and if

one of their followers has a problem, like he lost his job
and his wife split and his trailer burned all in the same
week, when do those preachers have time to go talk to the
poor soul?

I'm old-fashioned when it comes to preachers. I
grew up in a small Methodist congregation, and I got
used to preachers who were always there when you
needed them, who mowed the grass around the church,
and who even knocked down the dirt daubers' nests in
the windows of the sanctuary so the dirt daubers wouldn't
bother the worshippers while the preacher was trying to
run the devil out of town on Sunday mornings. Every
time I see Billy Graham on Meet the Press or catch Oral
Roberts or Jerry Falwell on the tube, I always wonder if
they have ever knocked down any dirt daubers' nests.
Every time I see any of those high-powered evangelists, I
also wonder whatever happened to Brother Roy Dodd
Hembree, who tried but never quite made it over the
hump into the land of evangelical milk and honey.

Brother Roy Dodd came to town every summer
when I was a kid with his traveling tent revival and his
two daughters, Nora and Cora. Nora was the better
looking of the two, but Cora had more sense. Nora would
do just about anything, including get bad drunk and then
tell her daddy what local bird dog had bought her the
beer. Brother Roy Dodd would then alert the sheriff's
office in whatever county he happened to be preaching in
at the time and demand the heathen buying Nora beer be
locked up for the duration of his revival as a means of
protecting his daughters.

Neither Nora nor Cora needed much protection, if the truth be known. Nora could cuss her way out of most any tight spot, and Cora had a black belt in switchblade.

Brother Roy Dodd's tent revival was the highlight of our summer, not only because of the opportunities Nora and Cora afforded, but also because Brother Roy Dodd put on a show that was in thrills and sheer excitement second only to the geek who bit the heads off live chickens at the county fair each fall.

They said Brother Roy Dodd was from over in Alabama and he used to be a Triple-A country singer until he got messed up with a woman one night in a beer joint where he was singing. The woman did a lot of winking and lip-pooching at Brother Roy Dodd during his act, and later, she told him her husband had gone to Shreveport to pick up a load of chickens and wouldn't be home until Saturday morning and there was still an hour or so left in Thursday.

Brother Roy Dodd, they said, knew there was trouble when, as he and the woman were in the midst of celebrating Friday night, he detected a poultry-like odor about the room. That was just before he heard two gunshots. Brother Roy Dodd caught one in each hip and it was shortly after the shooting, he found the Lord.

When he had recovered from his injuries, Brother Roy Dodd bought a tent and an old school bus and set out to spread the Word and his interpretation of it with a Bible he borrowed from his hospital room.

One night in Palatka, Florida, Brother Roy Dodd converted fourteen, including a young woman who had done some winking and lip-pooching of her own during the service.

After the service, Brother Roy Dodd confirmed the fact his winking and lip-pooching convert had no husband nor any connection with the business of transporting chickens, and asked the young woman if she would like to leave Palatka behind her. She consented and they said Brother Roy Dodd married himself to her, standing right there in the sawdust.

Her name was Dora. Hence, Nora and Cora. Dora learned to play piano and accompany Brother Roy Dodd when he sang the hymn of invitation each night, "Just As I Am (Without One Plea)," but Nora and Cora strayed early. Nora was smoking when she was nine, drinking when she was eleven, and she ran off one night with a sawmill hand from Boaz, Alabama, when she was thirteen, but came back three weeks later, with his truck and the $50 he gave her to leave.

Cora was a couple of years younger than Nora and they said she had taken after her daddy as far as music went, but she had a wild side, too, and learned how to knife fight the year she spent in reform school when she was fourteen. Her crime was lifting the wallet out of a deputy sheriff's trousers, the pair he shouldn't have taken off in the back seat of his cruiser out behind the tent one night during a revival near Swainsboro, Georgia.

My older cousin took me to see Brother Roy Dodd the first time. I was nine. My cousin was sixteen and he had a car. Everybody else came to find the Lord. My cousin came to find Nora and Cora, which he did. I said I could find a ride home, and the next day, he told me how Nora had taken drunk later that night and how Cora had tried to cut a man for looking at her wrong.

"I never heard such cussing as Nora did," my cousin said.

"You ought to have heard her daddy," I said.

I had never heard anybody speak in tongues before I heard Brother Roy Dodd. He was up in front of everybody and he was rolling forth out of Galatians, when, suddenly, he was caught in the spirit.

His eyes rolled back in his head and his voice boomed out through the tent:

"ALIDEEDOO! ALUDEEDOO! BOOLEYBOO-LEYBOOLEYBOO!"

"Praise God, he's in the spirit!" said a woman behind me.

"Praise God, he is!" said her husband.

"Don't reckon Brother Roy Dodd's sick, do you?" asked another man, obviously a first-timer.

Brother Roy Dodd tongue-spoke for a good six or eight minutes before the spirit finally left him and he went back to talking so you could understand what he was saying.

Brother Roy Dodd explained that the "tongue" was a gift only a blessed few received. I asked the Lord to forgive me, but I was deeply hopeful at that moment I would never be so blessed. I was afraid I might get in the spirit and never get out.

A couple of years later, there was some more excitement at Brother Roy Dodd's revival. In the middle of one of Brother Roy Dodd's sermons, a man stood up in the back and shouted, "Brother Roy Dodd! Have you ever taken up the serpent?"

Brother Roy Dodd said he hadn't.

"Would you take up the serpent to prove your faith?" asked the man.

"Never been asked to," answered Brother Roy Dodd.

"Well, I'm asking you now!" bellowed the man, who rushed toward the pulpit with a wrinkled brown sack in his hand. He dumped the contents of the sack at Brother Roy Dodd's feet and the crowd gasped. Out of the sack came a cottonmouth moccasin of some size. The snake did not appear to be overjoyed with the fact it was currently involved in a religious experience.

I knew all about taking up the serpent. It had been in the papers. There was a sect that believed a certain passage of the Bible beseeched a man to hold a snake to prove his faith. The papers had a story about a man who had been bitten recently by a timber rattler during services over at a church in Talbot County. The faithless scoundrel nearly died.

Brother Roy Dodd wasted little time in dealing with the snake. He picked up a metal folding chair in front of the piano, the one his wife Dora had vacated immediately upon seeing the snake, and beat hell and guts out of it.

When the snake was no longer moving, Brother Roy Dodd picked it up and held it before the stunned crowd.

"Shame I didn't have a chance to save this belly-crawling sinner before the Lord called him home," said Brother Roy Dodd.

The crowds began falling off for Brother Roy Dodd as the years passed. He added a healing segment to his performance to try to pick things up.

Miss Inez Pickett, a stout woman in her late fifties, came to see Brother Roy Dodd one night, complaining of what women used to call "the old mess," some sort of kidney disorder that was usually only whispered about.

Brother Roy Dodd, dressed in a sequin jacket he'd held on to since his singing days, asked Miss Inez where it hurt.

"My back," said Miss Inez.

Brother Roy Dodd put his hands firmly on Miss Inez's back and shook her kidneys with great force as he prayed.

"Did you feel that, Sister Inez?" asked Brother Roy Dodd.

"Lord Godamighty, I think I did!" shouted Miss Inez.

"You're healed!" said Brother Roy Dodd.

Miss Inez, plagued by her infirmity for many years, bounded about the platform in the manner of a much younger woman and made a number of joyful noises. I was afraid she was going to break into tongue.

Instead, she fell off the platform in her excitement, and you could hear the bone snap in her leg.

"Somebody call an ambulance!" the first one to her said.

"No need to do that," said somebody else. "Just get Brother Roy Dodd to give her another healing."

"Don't do no broke bones," said Brother Roy Dodd. "Just vital organs."

I was sixteen the summer Brother Roy Dodd didn't come back anymore. We heard all sorts of things. Nora and Cora left him for good, they said. Dora, his wife, got sick and couldn't play piano anymore. There was even something about a sheriff down in Mississippi someplace finding some white liquor on Brother Roy Dodd's bus.

That was a long summer, that summer Brother Roy Dodd didn't come back. We just sort of sat around and waited for fall and the fair and the geek who bit the heads off live chickens.

* * * *

Talking to my preacher was my last order of business before getting on with the matter of the surgery on my heart.

I had heard all the statistics. Emory Hospital's most recent figures concerning heart surgery were quite favorable. The mortality rate was under three percent, and that included those who went to the table in desperate conditions.

One of my doctors had also assured me of the relative safety of the operation. He said there is always the unknown factor, but in many ways, when a person goes through surgery, he or she is safer than at any other time of his or her life because every part of the body is being closely monitored.

I was only thirty-five. They had called me an "excellent surgical risk." Still there was no absolute guarantee I might not wind up Emory's Upset Special of the Week, so I did, in fact, have to deal with the possibility my end might be near.

I had my will drawn up before I went to the hospital. Wills always begin by making reference to the fact the person about to dole out his life's belongings in the event of his demise is sound of mind. A person with complete control of his faculties wouldn't do such a thing in the first place.

Making out a will is depressing. I'll be honest. When it comes down to it, you really do want to take it with you.

Take my red coat. The Christmas before, I received the gift of a red, ultra-suede sports jacket. I don't know exactly where I was supposed to wear a red, ultra-suede sports jacket since I don't attend Shriners' conventions, but it was a rather spiffy jacket, nonetheless.

I had shown it to a friend earlier, who was quite impressed.

"Wish I had a coat like that," he said.

"Where would you wear it?" I asked, just for the record.

"Next Shriners' convention," he said.

My friend came to visit soon after he found out about my impending heart surgery.

"Don't worry about a thing," he said. "People go through these operations all the time. It's a piece of cake."

You would be surprised how many people told me how easy heart surgery was going to be before I went in to have heart surgery. Most of them, incidentally, had

95

never been through medical procedures any more serious than offering a urine specimen.

"Still got that red coat?" my friend asked. I began to catch his drift.

"Still got it," I said. "Why do you ask?"

"Well, you never know about these things. I was just thinking that if you didn't make it through—not that there's one in a million chances you won't—maybe I could have your red coat."

One thing I made certain of in my will. Nobody got my red coat in case I bought the farm during my heart surgery. I left strict instructions I be buried in it.

My minister and I were alone in the hospital room. I was stretched out on the bed. He pulled his chair alongside me. A good preacher has a way about him, a way that calms.

First, we had a long discussion about hell. Hell has always confused me. Who goes to hell? Hitler, of course. Bonnie and Clyde must be there. There was a man in my hometown who shot at dogs for sport. My cousin had a fluffy little dog named Snowball and the man shot my cousin's dog dead.

"I hope he burns in hell for shooting my dog," said my cousin.

"On the same spit with Hitler and Bonnie and Clyde," I added.

As a kid, I always wondered exactly where hell was. Heaven is up; hell is down. But down where?

I used to wonder if you could dig your way to hell. I asked my minister about it.

"You probably can," he agreed. "But there are quicker ways to get there."

That brought up the current state of my status with the Lord.

"I haven't exactly been faithful," I said.

"None of us have," said my minister.

"I don't think you understand," I went on. "At last count, I had violated eight of the original Ten Commandments and had strongly considered the other two."

My preacher talked about forgiveness. He talked about it for a long time. Brother Roy Dodd couldn't have explained it any better. I listened closely. When he finished, I said, "Then you think if I don't make it through the operation tomorrow, there's still time for me to be forgiven for all the things I've done wrong?"

He looked at his watch.

"There's still time," he said, "but I'd get on it right away."

We prayed together before he left. He asked God to watch over me during the operation. I wanted him to ask God to have a sense of humor when he looked over my past life, but he didn't ask that.

I got out of my bed as the preacher began to leave. Family and friends were outside waiting.

First, I shook his hand. Then, I reached my arms around him, and he reached his arms around me.

Compared to the comfort and assurance of resting in the loving arms of a man of God for a few moments, Valium is child's play.

VII

Adventures in ICU

THE HEAD NURSE came into the room at ten o'clock and asked everyone to leave. Everyone except me, of course. This was the part of the pre-surgery period I had dreaded the most. I said my goodbyes.

"You're sure about your red coat?" asked my friend, the Shriner.

"Positive," I said.

My stepfather was there. He's a good man who married my mother when I was ten and who has looked after her all these years and who is solid in situations like these. My mother's own health problems had kept her from being with me.

"Tell Mother I love her," I said to my stepfather.

"I'll tell her," he said.

We shook hands. If I had it all to do over again, I would have hugged his neck.

I kissed my wife. I wanted to say something poetic, like if I didn't make it, I'd meet her just beyond the moon. I heard that line in a Tex Ritter song, believe it or not.

All I could say to her was, "Thanks for bringing the chili dogs." I guess I'm no Tex Ritter.

The nurse gave me another sleeping pill and turned out my light. It was dark. I was alone. The buses had stopped running at ten. I prayed one last time. All I could do now was let the drugs take my dreams and what was left of my fear.

* * * *

At six in the morning, another nurse brought me out of what had actually been a restful sleep with a gentle tug on my arm. She even had the morning newspaper. I read the sports section first. North Carolina was storming toward the collegiate basketball championship. There was a story about how lousy the Chicago Cubs were looking in spring practice.

That reminded me to look in my little bag I had brought with me from home. Something else I put in there I forgot to mention. I put in my lucky Chicago Cubs baseball cap I bought one day when I lived in Chicago and used to walk up to Addison and Clark Streets to Wrigley Field to watch the Cubs mostly lose.

The reason I figure a Chicago Cubs baseball cap is lucky is this: The Cubs haven't won a pennant since 1945. Season after season, they are a terrible disappointment to their followers. Yet, no Cub has ever been seriously injured by an irate fan, which is a minor miracle. Maybe, I concluded, it was the caps that kept the players from harm.

I put on my Cubs cap while the nurse scurried around my bed, taking my temperature and checking my blood pressure.

"What are you doing with that hat on?" she asked.

"It's not a hat," I replied. "It's a cap. Don't you know anything about baseball?"

"I don't care what it is," the nurse replied, "but you'll have to take it off when we take you out."

I hadn't counted on this.

"What's wrong with me wearing a cap when you take me out?" I inquired, a bit indignantly.

"You can't wear something like that into surgery because it can't be sterilized," she said.

Once a guy sitting behind me at Wrigley Field had tried for a foul ball and spilled his beer on my cap, but other than that, it was perfectly clean.

"I'm wearing my cap," I said.

"You want another enema?" asked the nurse.

I put my cap back in my bag and went into the bathroom to take my shower.

They give you a brush and medicated soap for your pre-op shower. The soap is yellow. Actually, it's caramel colored. Actually, it was the color of that lotion they came out with years ago called "Q.T." for "quick tan." The idea was to spread it over your body and it would give you an instant tan without you ever having to set foot into the hot sun. The problem, of course, was that it was impossible to spread the lotion over your body evenly, so you wound up looking like a pinto pony.

What you are supposed to do is scrub that soap all

over your body with the brush. The brush has very brittle teeth, and your body, having been shaved the night before, is very tender. When I finished my shower, my body felt like the entire Chicago Cubs infield had just walked across it wearing their cleats.

There was something that had been worrying me about this particular moment. I did not relish the idea of being conscious when they rolled me into the operating room. I didn't want to see it. I didn't want to see the table. I didn't want to see the operating team. I didn't want to see the table of instruments. I was also afraid they might have the little pig in there who was donating the valve. I didn't want to come face to face with the pig, either.

No problem. The nurse gave me another Valium, a whammo dosage. I began to drift off. I barely remember what came next. What came next was a shot in my rear to take me even farther out.

I have no recollection whatsoever of leaving my hospital room. As a matter of fact, I have no recollection whatsoever of the next eight or so hours. I can reconstruct it here only through later conversations with those involved in my operation and in my immediate post-operative care.

At 6:45 A.M., they wheeled me out of my hospital room toward the surgical unit. I was carrying on, they said, but nobody was exactly certain what I was carrying on about. Everything was normal so far.

Before entering the operating room, I was taken to what is called a holding room. It was 7:15. Further preparation was made for the surgery. EKG leads were put into place. Small lines were placed in various arteries for measuring pressures.

At 8 A.M., I was taken into the operating room. More lines and tubes. One anesthetic ended my senseless carrying-on and put me even farther out. Another blocked nerves in order to relax my body. More tubes, including the one tube I had worried about the most. The one to my bladder.

"We always wait until the patient is all the way under before we put in that catheter," a doctor told me later. I would like to go on record as thanking the medical profession for that concession to the comfort of their patients.

There were eight other people in the room besides the one sound asleep with the bladder catheter in him. Three on the surgical team, two anesthesiologists, a nurse assisting, a nurse circulating, and two to run the heart-lung machine.

My body was covered with sterile drapes. The lines and tubes were in place. The surgeon took his scalpel and made the initial incision into my skin. He started just below the base of my neck and went just below my sternum, four inches above my navel. Something to know about having heart surgery. Very little muscle tissue is cut when the incision is made. That cuts down on painful muscle spasms that cause so much discomfort following surgery to other parts of the body.

This is the part that still gives me the creeps: After the skin incision is made, the surgeon takes in hand what

105

is known as a Stryker saw. It is an oscillating saw that cuts through the breastbone. I was told it cuts through the bone very cleanly and doesn't make a lot of noise, so do not think about the movie, *The Texas Chain Saw Massacre,* as you read this.

Once they had cut through my breastbone, a chest retractor was used to open a large area in my chest in order to give the surgeons room to work. My ribs buckled in the process. This creates a great deal of discomfort following surgery, but at least the doctors have room to use both hands.

Then came the stickiest part of the procedure. The reason it is possible to make necessary repairs to the heart today, is the development of the heart-lung machine. They explained to me the details of how it works, but here is about all I understood.

The heart must be stopped so the surgeon can do his work. The heart is stopped by cooling it. The entire body of the patient is cooled to twenty-eight degrees centigrade (eighty-two, fahrenheit), as a matter of fact, which reduces the metabolism of the heart and also reduces the amount of oxygen it needs, a safeguard against further damage to the heart muscle during the surgery.

A tube is inserted into the aorta on the left side of the heart, and then two more tubes are inserted into the right side. Blood then actually bypasses the heart through the tubes and flows into the heart-lung machine, which oxygenates it and filters it and circulates it throughout the body.

The heart is not beating. It is clear of blood. But the

surgeon is able to work on a live patient because of that marvelous machine that is taking the place of the patient's heart and lungs.

A clamp was placed on my aorta, the artery leading from the left ventricle of my heart. My aorta was then opened and the surgeons looked in at the valve for the first time.

The leaflets of my valve, I was told later, were elongated and thin from overwork and were falling back into my heart chamber.

The leaflets of my original valve were taken out. Fifteen sutures went in to hold the new valve, which had arrived in the operating room without its original owner, I was assured later.

I received a twenty-seven millimeter, Carpentier tissue valve, produced by American Edwards Laboratories, Model No. 2625, Serial No. AB0574. (I never did get the hog's name.) The valve I received was comparatively large. The larger the better. The problem with tissue valves is if and when they begin to deteriorate, they also begin to shrink. Larger valves have farther to shrink before there is trouble and blood leakage begins all over again.

One other note. No incisions were actually made into the muscle of my heart. The work was done on the outside where the valve meets the aorta. I did not then undergo "open heart surgery" and neither do most other heart surgery patients. Coronary bypass surgery, the most common sort of heart surgery today, for instance, requires no entrance into the heart chamber itself. "Open

107

heart surgery" is what the guy down the street always thinks you had. So let him think that. It sounds more exotic than just heart surgery, anyway.

Once the valve is in place, the heart is warmed again and all electrical activity re-starts. The patient comes off the bypass of the heart-lung machine, the most critical period is over. What is left to do is put his chest back together again.

The sternum is closed with heavy stainless steel wire that grows into the core of the bone. This causes no pain afterwards, but when you have chest X-rays taken later, it looks like you swallowed a box of paper clips.

As far as putting the skin back together, I got lucky. My surgeon practices a method whereby the sutures run underneath the skin surface so your chest doesn't look like a football. My scar, as a matter of fact, looks like I was stealing eggs and the chicken scratched me. Nobody who sees my scar is the slightest bit repulsed by its appearance, not even strangers I stop on the street.

The actual procedure of opening my chest, diverting my blood to the heart-lung machine, replacing my valve, taking me off bypass, and closing my chest back again took fifty-one minutes.

There were no problems. No complications. Damn good surgical team.

* * * *

There is nothing for family and friends to do but wait. The hospital was kind enough to provide a private

108

waiting area. They wouldn't allow the two witch doctors in, however. I paid two witch doctors fifty bucks each to dance and chase away any evil heart-surgery spirits that might have been lurking within a twenty-five-mile radius of DeKalb County, Georgia. They also made the girls' drum and bugle corps I had hired wait in the parking lot. They were to hit it when word came I had survived the operation. You cover all the bases in a situation like this.

My senior cardiologist, a learned and kind and gentle man, kept those who love me most posted on my progress.

He told them when I went on the bypass machine. He told them when the surgery was over. I understand the subsequent celebration set no records, but the girls' drum and bugle corps was well into their third number in the parking lot before somebody called the cops.

My secretary waited in my office. She was given the word the surgery had been a success. She was to pass it on to the thousands who would be calling in.

I asked her later how many people actually called.

"Two," she said.

"Two thousand?"

"No, two, period. One was from an old friend calling long distance. He wanted to know if you had lived."

"And what did you tell him?"

"I told him you were alive, but you didn't know it yet."

"Who else called?"

"The captain of your league tennis team."

"What did he say?"

"Well, after I told him you were okay, he said, 'Now what in the hell am I going to do with a dozen black armbands?' "

After the surgery was completed, I was taken to the Coronary Intensive Care Unit where a tube was inserted into my throat and down into my lungs. This is called a respirator tube. It does your breathing for you until your lungs can shake off the effects of the anesthetic and the effect of inactivity while the patient is on the heart-lung machine. It is during this period the lungs fill with fluids.

My family and friends were allowed into my room in the Intensive Care Unit soon after I arrived there.

"I thought you were dead," my wife told me later.

"You were cold and white as a sheet," said my stepfather.

"I've seen you look worse only one other time," said one of my friends.

When I had the Asian flu and was in bed for a week?

"No, the morning after you drank the bottle of tequila at the beach and ate the three dozen raw oysters and we found you asleep with your head in the john."

I remember that. I was so sick I wanted to drown myself, but I knew I could never make it to the ocean, so I tried the nearest available body of water.

Let's go back to the respirator tube. They had told me about the respirator tube the day before my surgery.

"We will put in a respirator tube following the surgery. When you first awaken, there will be some discomfort. We will have to restrain your arms because some patients have been known to attempt to remove their respirator tubes."

The first thing I did when I regained consciousness following my surgery was to attempt to remove my respirator tube. There's that medical understatement again. "Some discomfort." Sheer terror.

I opened my eyes and I tried to do something very simple like take a breath. I couldn't take a breath. I tried to take another breath. Nothing. I panicked. I was very much aware of the respirator tube. This, I reasoned, was what was responsible for my inability to breathe.

I tried to reach to my mouth and pull the respirator tube out of my body and throw it at whomever was responsible for putting it there. I had forgotten the part about my arms being restrained.

I looked around me. One of my friends was standing to the left of me. Thank God, I thought. He will get this thing out of my throat so I can breathe. I tried to say, "Get this thing out of my throat so I can breathe!" to my friend.

Something else they had told me that I had forgotten. You can't talk with a respirator tube in your throat because they shove it down through your voice box. I made a mental note to discuss this with my witch doctors later, in the event I managed to somehow survive this obvious attempt to kill me. Somebody was going to by-God pay for this little trick.

Then I remembered they had also told me if I wanted to communicate during the time the respirator tube was in my throat, there would be a tablet and pencil near my right hand and I could write out what I wanted to say.

I felt for the tablet and pencil. Nothing. I had one last chance. I reached my right hand as high as it would reach with the straps around my arm and I tried to write out certain words in the air.

"Look," said my friend at my left, "he's trying to tell us something."

"What do you think he's trying to say?" asked my wife, who was standing nearby.

"I think he's trying to say hello."

"How cute," said my wife.

I wasn't trying to say hello. I was trying to say I had about eight seconds to live and don't just stand there like a couple of raw oysters, get this blessed tube out of my throat.

Finally, a nurse got the message.

"He doesn't think he can breathe," she said. "It happens to everybody."

She peered over my bed and looked squarely into my fear-stricken eyes.

"Just relax," she said. "The tube is doing your breathing."

I reached my hand up again and tried to write, "You wouldn't kid me, would you?" in the air.

"He'll go back to sleep in a minute," I heard the nurse say.

Some patients keep the tube longer than others. Some patients' lungs clear up more quickly than others. If a patient is a smoker, he can keep that tube down his

112

throat for twenty-four hours or more. On May 10, 1980, I had given up smoking.

When I awakened for the second time, four or five hours later, the tube was out of my throat and I could breathe on my own. I couldn't reach down there and pull in a big gulp of air because of all the diddling around that had been done in my chest, but what little breath I could manage never felt better.

I vividly recall the thought I had at this marvelous moment: They ought to burn every tobacco field still standing.

VIII

Tubes

FRANKLY, I WOULD like to end any further discussion of tubes at this point, but tubes are what heart surgery is all about, especially after the patient reaches the Intensive Care Unit where the tubes begin to come out.

There are seven places on the human body where a tube may be inserted without making a new hole. (I'll wait a second while you count.) I don't think God had any intention for anybody to go sticking tubes, or anything else, in at least a couple of those holes, but they stick tubes there anyway when they operate on your heart.

I'm not certain the exact number of tubes they eventually stick in you before, during, and after heart surgery, but it is considerably more than seven, which means they have to make some new holes. Just north of your navel, they make two, one to the east and one to the west, and that's where your chest tubes go.

I wasn't aware of it when they made the chest tube holes in my stomach because I was under the anesthetic at that point. Nobody would have made chest tube holes in my stomach, otherwise, because as a small boy growing up in the rural South, I learned if anybody came at you with something sharp with the intention of making new holes in you, you ran away as fast as you possibly could and called the local authorities and reported somebody was trying to cut you, which was against the law in my county unless it could be proved the victim needed cutting.

One morning after I had regained some of my senses in ICU, I was relaxing with a jar of morphine when a doctor I had never seen before walked casually into my room, whistling.

"I'm going to remove your chest tubes," he said, once he had stopped whistling.

My chest tubes, I had been told earlier, were for the purpose of drainage. Some tubes they use to put things into you. Others they use to take things out. Fully-tubed, a heart surgery patient bears a great deal of resemblance to the distributor cap of a 1956 Plymouth Fury.

It hurt. Morphine or no morphine, the removal of my chest tubes was the worst thing that happened to me during the entire experience of having heart surgery.

"You okay?" asked the doctor once he had removed the tubes.

"Get away from me," I said.

I felt like he had snatched my innards from their very holdings.

"Come back here with my pancreas!" I screamed at the doctor as he left the room, whistling again. I didn't even get his tag number.

118

I will never forget how it felt to have my chest tubes removed. Now, every time I hear a whistling sound, I double up into a tight knot and fall on the floor and lie very still, which is a problem only when I am driving in heavy traffic and the radio station to which I am tuned tests its Emergency Alert System.

The chest tube experience did have its value, however, and that was to assure me that I had lived through the operation. You can't be dead and hurt that badly at the same time.

After the chest tube horror, I began to count the other tubes that were running in and out of my body. I started with the one in my neck. That is called a Swan-Ganz Catheter. It measures various pressures in the body. Find a pressure somewhere and somebody in a hospital is going to want to measure it, even if it means sticking a tube in your neck.

There were also needles and lines in my arms and wrists. I was being fed through one. Given a choice between eating the lunch they had served me my first day in the hospital and getting food from a bottle through a tube and a needle, I'd go for the bottle and the tube and the needle every time. At least there was no chewing involved.

Another line was for the morphine to kill pain. Except for when somebody wants to pull a tube out of your stomach, the pain immediately following heart surgery is quite bearable, as long as you lie perfectly still.

There was another tube in my rectum to measure my temperature. Why the rectum is a good place to measure a person's temperature is beyond me, but at least it doesn't take a large tube to do the job, which is something for which I was quite grateful.

I also noticed some small wires that had been attached to my stomach. They were pacemaker wires. In case there arose the need to alter my heartbeat, the wires could be used to send electrical impulses to my heart. They mess your stomach up pretty good when they operate on your heart.

Then, of course, there was the bladder catheter, and we all know where they stick that. I couldn't bear to look at where they had stuck my bladder catheter.

All around me were machines with dials and screens and things making beeping noises.

"Every part of your body is being monitored," a nurse told me.

She was a very pretty nurse, with dark hair and when she walked around in my room in her snug nurse's outfit, I found myself monitoring certain parts of her body.

"Do me a favor," I said to her.

"What's that?"

"Walk past me again and let's see if the machine beeps louder."

She did and it did, and I felt quite comfortable in the assumption heart surgery hadn't affected my capacity for lust, even with the aforementioned tube the size of a small garden hose intruding in the situation.

In Intensive Care, one by one, the tubes began to come out. The chest tubes went by the hand of the

120

whistling doctor. The nurse took out the Swan from my neck. The lines came out of my arms and wrists. No problem.

Then, one morning the nurse pulled back the sheet and announced it was time to remove the bladder catheter.

"And you're going to do it?" I asked.

"I do this all the time," she said.

The stories she must have.

It wasn't all that bad, compared to the removal of the chest tubes. The nurse gave the tube a tug and out it came with nothing more than a slight sting. I still couldn't bear to look, however.

"Everything seem to be in order?" I asked her with a slight halt in my voice.

"Little fellow's looking just fine to me," she answered.

You'd think a nurse with that much experience in such matters would have elected to use a better choice of words.

Before I left ICU, the cough lady came to see me. I don't know her official title, but she came into my room and explained that it was time I got out of my bed, sat myself down in a chair and coughed.

"You need to cough up the fluids in your lungs," she said.

She helped me out of the bed to the chair. My first steps were slow. I was dizzy, for one thing. I figured I still wasn't over the chili dogs.

After I had sat down in the chair, the lady brought

121

me a pillow and said to hold it to my chest as tightly as I could.

"This will ease some of the pain when you try to cough," she explained.

She even told me how to cough.

"Take as deep a breath as you can take and then cough several times as hard as you can. Like this . . ."

She took a keep breath, clutched the pillow and made a sound like somebody trying to crank a pulpwood truck on a cold morning.

"HRRRACK! HRRRACK! HRRRRACK!" went the cough lady.

I took a deep breath and squeezed the pillow to my chest. I didn't go "HRRRACK!" at all. I barely made a sound.

"You've got to try harder," said the cough lady.

I tried again, but I didn't try any harder. I knew if I tried any harder, it would hurt and no stupid pillow would make it stop.

The cough lady came back two or three more times and tried to get me to do a couple of hrrracks. I never did the first one.

"You don't smoke?" she asked.

"Gave it up two years ago."

"Smokers have to do a lot of coughing after their surgery. I guess you don't have any fluids left in your lungs."

"I won't tell anybody if you won't," I said.

The cough lady left and went to bother somebody else.

122

* * * *

I was very pleased to get out of Intensive Care and back into a regular room in the coronary wing. The only thing still attached to my body that hadn't come attached in the first place were the pacemaker wires on my stomach. My first morning out of ICU another doctor I had never seen came to take those out. He carried a pair of wire snippers. He snipped this wire and then that wire.

"Dang if you're not a bleeder," he laughed.

I looked at my stomach. It was very red.

I remained as still as possible and didn't say a word while the doctor finished. You don't risk arousing a man who thinks a stomach covered with blood is funny, especially if he is packing a pair of wire snippers at the time.

My cardiologist came in and checked my heart.

"Sounds just fine," he said.

A couple of his assistants came in and they listened to my heart, too.

"Outstanding," said one.

"Couldn't be better," said the other.

My blood pressure. They checked that, too. Before the surgery, the range had been extremely wide. I even recorded a two hundred over zero at one point.

After surgery, I was one-twenty over eighty. Perfect.

I looked at my scar. I had expected it to be much worse. There would also be two small scars from the chest-tube incisions, but once the hair grew back on my chest, they would be barely visible.

There was pain when I tried to get a deep breath, but nothing I couldn't handle. The area around my collarbone and my sides were sore from the chest retractor during surgery, but that wasn't so terrible, either.

I was still a big foggy from all the drugs, but I'd been foggier. Recall the tequila and oyster episode.

I had made it. The surgeons had plugged the leak in my heart, my blood pressure couldn't have been better, and my prior fear of being delirious with pain at this point had been a needless concern. I was in only mild discomfort.

All this presented a bit of a problem, however. You don't go through heart surgery and not expect a large portion of sympathy. If the doctors and nurses and my family and friends knew how good I really felt, they might not feel as sorry for me as I wanted them to feel, and they might not continue to wait on me hand and foot as I most certainly deserved.

I decided to do one of the things I do best in order to assure everyone involved I was in a most pitiable state. I decided to whine a lot.

I can whine with the best of them. I have different whines for different situations. There is my hangover whine.

"Ohhhhhhhhhhhhhh, my Gooooood!" is my basic hangover whine.

"I think I'm going to die," is the whine I use when I have a bad cold and I want somebody to bring me ginger ale and chicken noodle soup and a piece of carrot cake, which will cure a cold in a New York minute, as long as you can get somebody else to bring it to you.

When I really want some attention and sympathy, however, I use a whine that defies a spelling.

It's sort of "Oooooooooooh," but with some "Awwwwwwwwwww," and a kind of high-pitched "Uhhhhhhhhh" thrown in. Ever heard the sound a dog makes when you step on its tail? It's sort of like that, too, except a dog takes a little break between sounds. When I use this whine, I am steady and constant with it.

I use this whine in the dentist's chair, and I used to use it when my mother wanted me to go outside and pull weeds out of her flowers, and I tried it on a state patrolman once who had stopped me for speeding. The dentist always ignores me and so did the heartless state patrolman, but I still haven't pulled the first weed out of my mother's flower garden.

"How do you feel?" my wife asked me the first afternoon I was out of ICU.

I put the big whine on her.

"Bless your heart," she said.

A couple of guys from my tennis team came in to see me.

"How are you feeling?" one asked.

I let go a dandy.

"Let's get out of here," said the other. "He's giving me the creeps."

You would figure nurses would know better than to go for whining. They don't. There was one nurse from ICU who had been particularly sweet to me. She didn't stick any tubes in me and she didn't take any out, either. She came to see me in my room.

"Are you getting along okay?" she inquired.

Whine.

"Bless your heart," she said, adjusting the pillows under my head.

"Would you like for me to rub your face with a wet towel?" she asked.

"If you wouldn't mind," I said, meekly.

When I asked her if she would run down to the convenience store and pick up a couple of six-packs, she refused, however. Whining does have its limits.

Actually, I think I did my best whining at night. They may have lousy lunches at Emory Hospital in Atlanta, but they make terrific milkshakes. I would order a milkshake and then whine my way into a pain pill. After a couple hours sleep, I would awaken and roll over on my back and press the button to call the night nurse.

I never did see her face and I never got her name, but the night nurse was an angel, too.

"You need something?" she would ask me.

I'd whine yes.

"Water?"

I'd whine no.

"Back rub?"

I'd whine yes.

"That feel good?"

I'd whine another yes.

"Had enough?"

I'd whine another no.

The perfect woman, I decided, would own a beer joint and rub your back for as long as you wanted her to.

They made me get up out of my bed and walk once I was back in my room. I would walk up the hall and then back down it again. It got easier each time I tried it, although it was weeks before I could actually walk completely upright. Stooped over like that got me more sympathy, however.

They also made me wear white stockings, which were very tight and which were supposed to improve the circulation in my legs. They looked like what baseball players call sanitary hose. Every morning, the orderly would come into my room and put fresh stockings on me. One morning, he asked if I wanted to try putting on my own stockings. I whined my way out of that and even convinced him to go get me a newspaper.

I turned to the sports section first. North Carolina was even closer to the national basketball championship, and the Cubs still couldn't beat a team made up of night nurses.

* * * *

I received a lot of cards and flowers in the hospital. I also received some gifts. I have a friend who runs a men's clothing store. He sent me a shirt. It fit. Another friend sent me a caricature of myself ogling a nurse in a tight skirt. That fit, too. The only thing I do better than ogle is whine.

127

I also got candy and fruit baskets and jars of peanuts and boxes of pecans and a Valvoline T-shirt and cap, and one day they even delivered balloons to my room. Cards and flowers and gifts and balloons are nice. They say people give a damn.

A little girl of nine or ten or so occupied the room directly across from mine. I thought I had trouble. She had two faulty valves. They had both been replaced.

Crowds gathered in my room. We ate the fruit and nuts and we laughed amongst the cards and flowers and balloons.

The little girl was alone. One of the nurses told me about her. She was from a poor family in another state. Her mother hadn't accompanied her for the operation.

"She's frightened nearly to death," said one of the nurses, "but she hasn't whined once."

I got the message.

The nurses helped me out of my bed and I walked over to the little girl's room. Her eyes. That's where most of the fear was, in her eyes.

I asked her questions. She would only nod her answers.

"Do you have any brothers and sisters?" I asked.

She nodded yes.

"How many?"

I think she tried to count them in her head, but poor families run big, and it's tough to keep track of the exact number who are sharing your attempt to survive.

"Maybe now that you are well," I said, "you can run around and play with all your brothers and sisters."

Maybe that thought hadn't crossed her mind as yet. Her nod yes was a bit more enthusiastic than the others had been.

I went back to my room and got back into my bed. Somebody had tied my balloons so they hovered above my head. I have always liked balloons. They remind me of circuses and celebrations.

I called for a nurse and told her to take my balloons over and give them to the little girl. I don't deserve any applause for that. I should have thought of it earlier. Little girls with frightened and lonely eyes and bright, bouncing balloons deserve to be together.

IX

Heart II

SIX DAYS after my heart surgery, I was released from the hospital. Six days. Give it another ten years and they might have patients in for surgery in the morning and home in time for the evening news. The next time somebody asks me for a donation to the heart fund, I'm going to think about that and dig a little deeper.

(My total bill was somewhere in the neighborhood of $15,000, of which I had to pay very little because I had insurance. The next time you curse your insurance payments, think about that.)

I dressed myself in preparation to leave the hospital. Most everybody had caught on to my whining act by then.

One of the doctors gave me some last minute instructions. He told me to wait two weeks before I had sex and six weeks before I drove a car. Or was it the other way around? I was still a little foggy and the entire discussion confused me, so I just promised him that I wouldn't drive and have sex at the same time and let it go at that.

He told me not to lift anything heavy. I made him put that in writing.

I asked about tennis.

"Six weeks," he said, "and then start very slowly and don't try to hit any serves or overheads until three months. I don't want you tearing the wires out of your sternum."

"How well do you think I can play tennis after this surgery?" I asked the doctor.

"How well did you play before?" he asked me back.

Somehow, I knew he was going to say that.

The doctor also told me to take daily walks and to go to bed early at night and to avoid drinking a great deal of alcohol.

"What would you consider the maximum number of beers I should drink a day?" I inquired.

"Two," said the doctor.

"Draught okay?"

"Draught is fine."

As it turned out, I wasn't nearly as foggy as I had thought.

They rolled me out of the hospital in a wheelchair. I said I could walk, but they insisted I take the wheelchair. A photographer from my newspaper came to take a picture of me leaving the hospital. I waved to him from the wheelchair. It made a terrific picture in the paper the next day and was probably responsible for the other cards and flowers and fruitbaskets and huge plates of homemade brownies I received after I got home.

There was some adjustment. The walks were difficult after the first two hundred yards. So I adjusted and gave up the walking in about a couple of weeks.

There were psychological leftovers. I didn't feel the immediate relief that I thought I would feel once the operation was over and I was home again. There is all the anxiety that builds up before the surgery, but there is no recollection of the actual operation, whatsoever. For weeks afterwards, I would awaken mornings and not be certain whether or not the surgery had taken place. Eventually, I would get around to checking out my hairless chest with the purple scar down the middle to settle any doubt.

There was some itching as my hair grew back. The scar puffed. It was weeks before I would turn my body fully toward the shower and allow the water to pour directly onto my chest.

It was also a while before I could pull my shoulders all the way back and walk without a stoop. Even then, there was an unsettling pulling sensation in my breast-bone. I felt quite fragile for at least the first month to six weeks after the surgery. One night I dreamed a fat lady sat down on my chest. I avoided getting near any fat ladies after that.

The ability of the body to heal itself after trauma is amazing, though. After six weeks, there was no more pain to speak of, I could get a deep breath with little reminder of the surgery, and I even went back to hitting tennis balls.

After the third session of rallying back and forth from the base line, my tennis partner said, "You know, you're hitting the ball now a lot like you were hitting it before your surgery."

I still don't know what he meant by that.

I was back at my typewriter writing newspaper columns eight days after my surgery. Somebody said this once about writing a daily newspaper column: It's like being married to a nymphomaniac. The first two weeks it's fun.

But it's what I do for a living. I hate it. I curse it. But without it, I'm somebody else.

Some very nice things happened to me after I returned home. Newnan, Georgia, is the seat of the county where I grew up. Somebody put up a big board at the courthouse in Newnan and people signed it, wishing me a speedy recovery. When they brought it to my house and gave it to me, I didn't cry. When they left, I cried.

My mother was in the hospital herself the day of my operation. My cousin was at her bedside during the hours I was in surgery. My cousin later wrote me a long letter telling me some of the things my mother said about me that day.

One of the things my mother said about me was that I had been a good son. I cried again when I read that letter.

* * * *

It is still less than four months since the surgery as I write this. I have been back for several checkups. All the doctors agree the operation was a complete success.

Once, I had the pounding, pistol pulse. Now, even after exercise, I am barely aware of my heartbeat. I am taking only one medication, Digoxin, which takes some of the work load off the heart. X-rays show my heart is already beginning to shrink back to its normal size.

My heart continues to show evidence of a slight leakage, but that was to be expected. Replacement valves, no matter how large, still can't do the job of a healthy original. There is also the possibility of dangerous infections in the valve. The blood that does leak back into the heart tends to eddy and is not sent through the body's filtering process. I am to take antibiotics at the first sign of fever, or when I go to the dentist. The mouth, it seems, is very susceptible to starting infections in the blood.

And there remains the possibility that somewhere in my later life, my new valve will deteriorate to the point I will need a second operation. But give me a good ten or fifteen years with the valve I have and who knows how far this incredible art of heart surgery may have progressed?

It is still too early to tell what profound effects this experience will have on me. I think I am better for it, obviously physically and probably otherwise, but I would not recommend it as a way of making improvements on one's self until all other avenues, such as seeing a chiropractor or joining a couple of religious movements, have been exhausted.

I do sense a few minor changes, however. I'm not nearly as afraid of flying and snakes as I was before.

After heart surgery, flying and snakes become small concerns. And I'm getting around to noticing blue skies and children's laughter a little more often, and I don't get nearly as angry as I once did when I am standing in a check-out line at a grocery store and a woman in front of me waits until they give her a total to go digging through her pocketbook for her money, which can take forever because women carry everything in those pocketbooks, even spare parts for their station wagons. I'm just happy to be in the line at all.

The most interesting thing I learned about myself during all this was that during the weeks and days and hours before the surgery, when perhaps I stood closer to death than at any other time in my life, I felt no remorse about the fact I might die and miss doing something I hadn't done before. What struck me as most regrettable as I considered dying was the fact I might not get to go back and repeat some earlier experiences I had accepted as commonplace.

There were some ladies and girls I wanted to kiss on the mouth again. I wanted to watch Herschel Walker run with a football again. I wanted to see the sun come up in Venice and go down behind a cluster of tall pine trees in Georgia again. I wanted to hear Willie Nelson sing "Precious Memories" and watch a dog run toward me with his ears flapping behind him in the breeze and I wanted to take a fat bream off a hook and hit an overhead for a winner and squeeze the hand of a friend long lost and read the Sunday *Times* over Sunday morning coffee and take a first pull from a longneck

138

bottle of beer and put on clean underwear after a shower and see my mama smile. Again.

And now, thanks to so many good and talented and caring people, and barring any other unforeseen catastrophes that might befall me, I will.

There is just this one other thing. There is the matter of what to do about the current condition of my second heart. We all have two. One, to lub-dub and carry on the actual function of life. Another, to skip and flutter and occasionally break with the bitter and sweet that living life inevitably brings.

They don't write songs about the first heart, the one that can be repaired by surgical brilliance. "I Love You Sorta, Way Down in My Aorta." That would never fly. They write songs about the second heart, the one that fills up and runs over when you hug her close and kiss her and she hugs you and kisses you back and the seat covers nearly catch on fire. The one she stomps flat and empty when she runs off six months later with somebody named Junior Ledbetter.

There are a lot of songs that have been written about situations like that. If somebody hasn't written one called, "If My Heart Was a Pick-Up Truck, It Would Be a Quart Low," then they should.

I lost my first love. I lost my second. I've hurt for my mama. I've missed my daddy, and I'll even admit to crying over a good dog long gone to dog heaven where they never run out of raw wienies and the creeks are always cool.

And a couple of months after my surgery, my third

attempt at being married fell hard and quick, for reasons I'll probably be years trying to figure out. The only thing I'm absolutely certain about is nobody named Junior Ledbetter was involved.

"How's your heart?" they ask me now.

Too few probably ever understand my answer.

"One's better than ever," I reply, "but danged if that other sucker still doesn't have a ways to go."